Praise for
When Good People Hav[e...]

"Whether you are having an affair or are thinking about it, or your partner is having an affair, this book is for you. Kirshenbaum brings us practical steps for understanding affairs and utilizing the mistakes we make for a deeper healing. This book can help strengthen all our relationships."

> —Rabbi Ted Falcon, Ph.D., rabbi of Bet Alef:
> An Inclusive Spiritual Synagogue in Seattle
> and coauthor of *Judaism for Dummies*

"Kirshenbaum addresses the often painful question of whether good people can and do have affairs and provides methodical, insightful answers to this very disturbing dilemma. I highly recommend this book to anyone who has had an affair, been the object of an affair, or has thought of having an affair."

> —Arthur P. Ciaramicoli, Ed.D., Ph.D.,
> author of *Performance Addiction* and
> *The Power of Empathy*

"This book is brilliantly written for anyone entrapped in a messy affair. Powerful, pragmatic answers clarify how to sanely address infidelity."

> —Lee Raffel, M.S.W.,
> author of *I Hate Conflict!*

"Kirshenbaum meets us right at the heart of an illicit affair and juggling two lovers. Her research and experience show most people who have affairs want what's best for everyone involved. Her absolute acceptance and wisdom teach us how we can trust ourselves, despite feeling crazy, to untangle our love triangles and live with choices that are free of regret and ambivalence. We can clearly decide what is good for us and what will lead to our happiness."

> —Diana Mercer, J.D.,
> attorney-mediator and founder of
> Peace Talks mediation services

"An important and insightful book on a very difficult topic."

—Gayle Rosenwald Smith,
author of *Divorce and Money*

"The 'sexual correctness police' surround us all the time and are so menacing we are often afraid to speak honestly and hence revert to humor to diffuse our anxieties. Mira Kirshenbaum has dared to break the rules, not by advocating for affairs (which too often are very destructive) but for acknowledging that they are happening, and giving advice to minimize the hurts and maximize the capacity of people to treat the others involved with the dignity and honesty they deserve."

—Rabbi Michael Lerner,
editor of *Tikkun* magazine and chair of the
Network of Spiritual Progressives

"Every pastor, therapist, and counselor should read this book. Mira Kirshenbaum, thanks to decades of clinical experience, demystifies affairs with wisdom, humor, buckets of common sense, and most of all, deep compassion for all involved. She provides from every perspective, including the children's, clear guidelines for decision making and the follow-through necessary for a long and healthy relationship. This book resonates profoundly with my thirty-eight years of ministering with people in relationships. Even the happily married would benefit from reading *When Good People Have Affairs*."

—M. Thomas Shaw,
member of the order Society of St. John the Evangelist
and bishop of the Episcopal Diocese of Massachusetts

"Mira Kirshenbaum has done it again! She has tackled the most difficult of issues and in so doing offers the reader clear and powerful tools for moving on and through the complexities of an affair. Every psychotherapist in the field knows that working with people involved in affairs is painful for all concerned. These are not bad people, as it would be too easy to assume. These are good people working through complicated issues, feelings, and needs. With steps for identifying why and then what next, this book will serve not only those who are personally involved with affairs, but also those in the helping role. I look forward to having it available as a recommendation for clients and as an aide in my own psychotherapy practice."

—Dr. Dorothy Firman,
director of the Synthesis Center (Amherst, Massachusetts)
and coauthor of *Daughters and Mothers: Making It Work,*
Chicken Soup for the Mother & Daughter Soul,
Chicken Soup for the Soul: Celebrating Mothers & Daughters, and
Chicken Soup for the Father & Son Soul

"If you've found yourself caught up in a love triangle, from any angle, Kirshenbaum provides an indispensable guide to what the person in two relationships is dealing with. If you are that person, this book will save you from a world of misery and help you do what's best for everyone. If you're the spouse or lover, this is a necessary guide to help you survive and thrive in the face of what you are really dealing with."

—Gay Hendricks, Ph.D.,
author of *Five Wishes* and coauthor,
with Kathlyn Hendricks, of *Conscious Loving*

"The first practical, nonjudgmental solution to infidelity. Kirshenbaum's ability to bring clarity out of a deeply confusing issue is amazing. This book is a must-read for the 50 percent of Americans whose lives have been affected by infidelity. It could save many relationships."

—Val Jones,
senior medical director of RevolutionHealth.com, and
author of the *Dr. Val and the Voice of Reason* blog

"Mira Kirshenbaum gives voice to the women and men who find themselves involved in an affair. With compassion and wisdom, she challenges the reader to understand and cope with his or her own infidelity. Asking difficult and incisive questions, she expertly guides the reader through the complex decisions that need to made in the aftermath."

—Constance Ahrons,
author of *The Good Divorce* and *We're Still Family*

"These are very needed words of wisdom. Important reading for anyone about to make a decision after the affair."

—Cloé Madanes,
author of *Strategic Family Therapy*, and cofounder, robbinsmadanes.com

"Mira Kirshenbaum's latest book delivers on its promise of a refreshing perspective . . . an open-minded and open-hearted view of what to do in the midst of what is often an overwhelmingly complex dilemma."

—Kathy Reiss, chaplain

WHEN
GOOD
PEOPLE
HAVE
AFFAIRS

ALSO BY MIRA KIRSHENBAUM

Too Good to Leave, Too Bad to Stay

Is He Mr. Right?

The Weekend Marriage

Our Love Is Too Good to Feel So Bad

Everything Happens for a Reason

The Emotional Energy Factor

Parent/Teen Breakthrough

Women & Love

The Gift of a Year

WHEN
GOOD
PEOPLE
HAVE
AFFAIRS

*Inside the Hearts & Minds of People
in Two Relationships*

MIRA KIRSHENBAUM

ST. MARTIN'S GRIFFIN

NEW YORK

www.stmartins.com

Book design by Ellen Cipriano

THE LIBRARY OF CONGRESS HAS CATALOGUED THE HARDCOVER EDITION AS FOLLOWS:

Kirshenbaum, Mira.
    When good people have affairs : inside the hearts & minds of people in two relationships / Mira Kirshenbaum.—1st ed.
    p. cm.
    ISBN-13: 978-0-312-37847-9
    ISBN-10: 0-312-37847-5
    1. Adultery. 2. Man-woman relationships. I. Title.

HQ806 .K485 2008
306.73'6—dc22

2008010390

ISBN-13: 978-0-312-56344-8 (pbk.)
ISBN-10: 0-312-56344-2 (pbk.)

10 9 8 7 6

*To all of us
who struggle so hard to find love,
who make so many mistakes, who feel so guilty,
and, in spite of it all, passionately want to do
what's best for everyone.*

CONTENTS

CONTENTS

FOURTH LEVEL ▪ DOING WHAT'S BEST FOR
THE CHILDREN

FIFTH LEVEL ▪ BREAKING UP THE TRIANGLE

SIXTH LEVEL ▪ HEALING THE PAST, BUILDING
A FUTURE

RESOURCES ▪ STUFF YOU NEED TO KNOW
ABOUT DIVORCE

ACKNOWLEDGMENTS

I'll tell you a secret. Are there other people around you right now? Maybe you're in a bookstore or waiting to board your plane or sitting on a beach. Most of these people, directly or indirectly, have been touched by an affair.

And these are the people I want to thank most for this book. Okay, maybe not the actual people you're looking at right now, but people just like them. People just like you and me.

These people have shared their stories and have opened their hearts to me. Over the years, many of them have been patients of mine. They've made it possible for me to see the inner workings of affairs from every possible vantage point. And I thank them with all my heart.

The stories they've shared are gripping. Much more important, though, is that they've made it possible for me to help a lot of people. Affairs happen, but it's how people handle the aftermath that determines the future of their relationships and their lives.

This is the very first book written from the point of view of the people who are having an affair. It's the very first book to get inside their minds and hearts. I thank all of them for their honesty.

For too long they've been the missing piece in the puzzle. Only by understanding them and helping them see how to do what's best for everyone can we begin to make the healing happen.

And I want to give thanks to the handful of people who told me not to write this book. I'm such a rebel—telling me I was about to enter forbidden territory just made me want to write it even more.

The lives of real people in real relationships have been the raw material of my professional life for many years now. This is what I know. My job is to take people as I find them and help them make themselves and their lives better. And I've learned that I can only help people if I approach them in an atmosphere of acceptance and love.

So I was relieved, but not surprised, by the encouragement I got from many people, especially the priests and rabbis I spoke to. In fact, it was actually members of the clergy most of all who supported me in offering the truth and help that's not been available before. Yes, we all agreed that infidelity is a sin and a mistake. But once you've crossed the line, what then? The clergy knows better than most people how much pain and suffering is connected with mishandling an affair, and how much the honest light of wisdom is needed.

I also need to thank my husband, Dr. Charles Foster. He is my full, fifty-fifty partner in writing this book and all of our books. Every word in this book is just as much his as it is mine. And he leads the research team here at the Chestnut Hill Institute.

As my agent, Howard Morhaim has been my partner in the white-water rafting experience that is publishing today. I couldn't have a better, more helpful, more loyal guide. Howard, you have my deepest gratitude. Many thanks also to Katie Menick, Howard's associate, who has been most kind to me and on top of things.

Danny Baror deserves my heartfelt thanks for bringing my ten books out in countries literally all over the planet.

Elizabeth Beier, my editor, has been great. Her energy, enthusiasm, and intelligence have meant a lot to me and this book. And

Elizabeth has turned out to be a wonderfully sympathetic, savvy editor. Many, many thanks.

A special thanks to Michelle Richter. And thanks to Sally Richardson for her thoughtfulness and help.

Thanks also to the great team at St. Martin's. The production editor was Julie Gutin, and she did a great job. The copyeditor was Rachel Burd, who really understood what I was trying to do and had a very sharp eye for all the ways I might have gotten into trouble. Special thanks to Colleen Schwartz, the publicist, and to Carrie Hamilton-Jones, who handles marketing, for bringing this book to people's attention so that everyone possible can benefit from the help that's in it.

Of course, I also have to thank my great team here at the Chestnut Hill Institute. Big thanks to Toby Desroches, Nikki Green, and Doc Miner for all the ways they help me and everyone else. You guys are the best. Special thanks to my incredibly talented webmaster, Christine Harbaugh.

And a big shout-out to all the people who, when I told them about this book, said, "Ooh, I can't wait to read it!"

■   ■   ■

If you have any comments or questions, if you need help, or if you just want to read my blog, please visit me at www.mirakirshenbaum .com.

INTRODUCTION

"YOU JUST DON'T HELP THOSE PEOPLE"

What shall we call them?

Not "cheaters." "Cheater" is a name for callous, mustache-twirling creeps and low-slung nymphomaniacs who are just trying to get away with something. It's a name for users. For sociopaths.

The men and women I'm talking about here are good people. *That's* what we should call them, because that's what they are. It's just that they're good people who made a mistake and got themselves into a complicated, messy, dangerous situation. They couldn't cope with one person, so they got involved with two! It's the last thing they ever thought would happen.

It's *because* they're good people that they lie awake at night feeling guilty and scared, wondering what to do. Wondering why this is happening to them. Wondering how to avoid hurting the people they care about and how to make sure their own needs don't get lost in the process. Wondering what's best for everyone. And trying desperately to figure out how to do what's best.

It's easy for bad people. They just focus on trying to make

themselves happy. But good people are concerned about everyone involved and end up feeling completely overwhelmed.

YOU TAKE PEOPLE WHERE YOU FIND THEM

Infidelity is a controversial topic. A friend of mine was pissed with me for taking it on. "You just don't help those people," she said.

Well, sure, if someone came to me and asked me to bless going ahead and starting an affair, I'd say don't do it—you'll cause more problems than you'll solve, and you'll hurt people you care about.

But people almost always come to me *after* they've already complicated their love lives. So what am I going to do, yell at them for having made a mistake? I wouldn't do that, just like if someone came to me with AIDS, I wouldn't yell at them for not practicing safe sex. You take people where you find them. And then you try to help them.

People who have affairs just want to find some real happiness and love in their lives. But they are opening up brand-new territory for themselves without a map or a compass. After all, infidelity can be anything from a passionate kiss with someone at a Christmas party to a full-blown relationship. Sometimes the attachment is mostly sexual. Sometimes—surprisingly often, in fact—the affair is mostly emotional. Sometimes it's with a stranger on the Internet; sometimes it's with a spouse's best friend.

So where do you draw the line? If your partner would feel hurt and betrayed by what happened, then it's infidelity.

WHY I WROTE THIS BOOK

I wrote this book because so many people came to me asking for help with this problem, and they had nowhere else to turn. The more research we did here at The Chestnut Hill Institute, the more people we interviewed, the more stories we uncovered, the more I realized that people in this situation need a lot of help, not just for their own sakes but for the sakes of everyone involved. Here is just some of what people told me they needed:

- To understand how a person "like me" could have gotten into a situation like this.
- To have a sense of how these kinds of things usually play out, and what all the issues are—sexual, emotional, and otherwise.
- To see clearly and confidently which of the two people they're involved with is the one they should be with.
- To know how to deal with all the feelings that come up in their situation—guilt, loneliness, depression, anxiety, shame, fear of loss.
- To know how to factor kids (if they have any) into the equation.
- To see how to handle the personalities and practicalities once they know which person they want to be with.
- To learn how to heal the relationship they end up in.

Until now, the story of these men and women has never been told. Shame and fear have kept it in the closet. And so they haven't had the understanding that might save them from ruining many lives.

Now things are different. We now know that we *can* help people understand how they got where they are—it turns out there are *seventeen* different reasons why people have affairs. We *can* help people make the best possible decisions for themselves and everyone they care about. And then we *can* help them do what has to be done in the healthiest possible way.

This is like being an emergency room doctor: Damage has been done, but you can still save lives and help people become whole again.

But I do understand how a lot of you feel about people who have affairs. Better than you might think.

I KNOW WHAT IT FEELS LIKE

You see once, a while back, my husband had a relationship with another woman. As far as I know—and believe me, I checked!—it wasn't a sexual relationship, and it didn't last very long. It was an emotional affair. But that didn't matter. It never does. It hurt me, and us, a lot. Affairs hurt everyone involved.

So does that leave me biased? You might think so. But here's what happened instead.

Like everyone in my situation, when my husband first confessed what had been going on, I felt violated, betrayed, devastated. I felt my whole marriage had been a lie, and that my husband had destroyed it.

So, sure, at first I hated my husband. Worse, I despised him. For a long time I thought he was a horrible person who'd done a horrible thing. Period.

But then the man I'd known for so many years started coming back into focus. He stood before me every day, and that person was a good person. I saw how sorry he was and how hard he was trying to make things better. So I had to deal with the head-exploding reality that he was a good person who'd done a horrible thing.

The problem is that good people don't do horrible things, I thought. Well, I eventually realized, maybe good people don't do horrible things, but they do make horrible mistakes. They get in over their heads.

And often they feel pushed into doing things they wouldn't do otherwise—a reality that made me look at the role I played in the whole mess. In fact, I wasn't blameless. I'd been overworked and felt undersupported, and I'd pushed him away.

Of course, I would never want anyone to go through anything like what I went through.

But I never want anyone to go through anything like what my husband went through, either.

MAKING US WHOLE AGAIN

You might be wondering if I have a hidden agenda here, such as trying to keep relationships together at all costs, or trying to break people up, or whatever. Well, I do have an agenda, and I'm happy to proclaim it openly. Call me a die-hard romantic, but my agenda is for everyone to find love—real love, lasting love.

And good people who have affairs share this goal. For them an affair may be the best way they know how to figure out what to do with love in their lives. It might be a mistake, but it's also an insight—something has been missing, something isn't working right, something needs to change.

Once it's begun, an affair can become a process by which people sort out their lives and—if they do it right—make their lives much better. The one thing good people who are having an affair say more than anything else is "I just want what's best for everyone." They really mean it, and if they handle things right, they can get it.

NO REGRETS

AFFAIRS COVER A LOT OF TERRITORY

Here's how Jessica, 37, put it: "In a million years I never wanted to be in a situation like this. To be in a committed relationship and then find myself having an affair—this just isn't me. But it *is* me. I've done this. And now I'm scared. All I wanted was to find some love, and now this whole thing could blow up, and I could lose everyone I care about."

People like Jessica, like most people having an affair, feel very much alone. But they're not. In fact, they've got plenty of company. As actress Sienna Miller said in a 2007 *Esquire* interview, commenting on her breakup from her boyfriend Jude Law following his affair with his kids' nanny, "Every single person I know has experienced infidelity. It's not the first time it's happened to me, and it probably won't be the last."

The research backs this up. (If you're a starry-eyed newlywed, get ready for a shock.) Based on all available surveys, in a near-majority of couples of all kinds (straight or gay) one or both partners will have an affair at some point. For example, 47 percent of married men are likely to get involved, emotionally and/or sexually, with someone else, as are 35 percent of married women (according to a 2007 Beta Research poll involving a representative sample of 1,738 randomly selected men and women ages twenty-one to forty-nine).

According to other surveys, more than half of single straight men ages twenty-five to fifty-five, and up to a third of single straight women ages twenty-five to forty-five, are involved with more than one person at the same time.

While there aren't yet good numbers on the size of this problem among gay men and lesbians, people in these communities typically say that it's just as big a problem for them.

Some are in their twenties, some—I assure you—are still lusty senior citizens, and the rest are somewhere in between. And it's not just that there are a lot of people involved; there's also a lot of variety in what goes on. Some people know for sure that they don't want to be with their partner but are paralyzed with fear that the breakup might hurt their kids. Some are utterly torn about who they really want to be with.

Sometimes the primary relationship is thoroughly awful, and sometimes there's just one piece missing.

So many people, so many messes. At some point, most good people having an affair wonder how they got into such a situation. They certainly didn't plan to be where they are.

How *does* an affair happen?

PORTRAIT OF AN AFFAIR

Let me paint a group portrait of the development of an affair. The details vary from person to person, of course. But, surprisingly, the same issues, events, and feelings keep coming up over and over, regardless of people's ages and backgrounds. Here is the general pattern.

It starts innocently. I know that's hard to believe, but it's usually true. When people say "I never meant for this to happen," they're being honest.

Typically they are in a committed relationship, but they aren't perfectly happy. No one who is perfectly happy in their primary relationship gets into a second. Maybe they're a lot unhappy, maybe just a little. Still, they have no plans to cheat.

And then "the other person" somehow floats onto their radar screen. It might be someone they work with every day. Or someone they've never met before whom they get into a conversation with while walking the dog or cooling down after yoga class.

Why they're attracted to this new person also varies. Sometimes it's just about the other person being good-looking. But much more often it's about how something that's been missing in their primary relationship, something they've been hungry for, suddenly seems possible with this new person. They're like someone who's been wandering around with a couple of empty wineglasses who suddenly meets someone with a bottle of wine.

IT STARTS. They only want a little taste. It might just be about sex. But my own research shows that even for men it's as likely to be about some other way of connecting. Usually it just feels good to talk to this person. Whatever it's about, part of them is attracted. But part of them is scared. Part of them says *never*.

Still, next thing they know . . . well, at this point there are a thousand and one scenarios.

Maybe, before they know it, before they even think about it, the two of them find themselves in bed making mad, passionate love.

Or maybe they very, very slowly get to know each other. Maybe they have long conversations about where the two of them are heading. Maybe they just play it by ear. Maybe they start out as friends and stay that way for quite a while.

However it happens, eventually they realize that they've crossed some sort of emotional or sexual line—*after* they've crossed it. And it feels wonderful, because, let's face it, it was a line they were hungry to cross. But it also feels terrible, because they know it's cheating, and they know that they never wanted to be a cheater.

But they are hungry and weak and confused, and so they keep going deeper into that new relationship.

KEEPING IT GOING. Now let's tell the truth. When they find themselves involved in two relationships, there is a point (it might last for just a minute, or it might last for months) when it looks as though this three-way state of affairs could work. Keeping the affair from their spouse seems doable. The guilt seems manageable.

They're not yet looking too closely at the future. They walk down the street feeling blessed by having a special secret, the key to a hidden wealth of happiness—sexual, emotional, whatever. They've somehow fallen into an eternal *now* that feels like a blessing, and seems to solve all their problems.

Unfortunately, as people always find out, that brief moment never lasts. It can't. Being in two relationships is inherently unsustainable. It's like a house of cards—the longer it keeps going, the more likely it is to come crashing down.

THE PRESSURE MOUNTS. Here's what good people at this stage of an affair do. As much as they can, they try to neither think about what's going on nor deal with it. They manage their life like a sleepwalker in traffic. This works until something crashes through and forces them to pay attention. And something always crashes through.

With every day, the risk of their spouse finding out grows. There are e-mail trails ("My partner just came across an e-mail that made him suspicious!"), unexplainable credit card receipts, stories made up that just don't hold water ("I told him we had a planning meeting at the office after work, but he came by to bring me something and found out that there was nobody there, and I had to explain that we'd all moved the meeting to a nearby restaurant").

Or maybe they've already been found out. This is a moment of great danger. A person has a better chance of surviving a heart attack than love has of surviving unscathed a discovery of infidelity. But then again, a lot of people survive heart attacks these days.

Still, it's very risky. There's a world of hurt and anger and mistrust to deal with. Certainly, having a spouse and a family puts enormous pressure on a person to end the affair.

Then again, maybe it's the lover who's applying intense pressure on someone to end their marriage. ("My lover wants me to spend some time over Christmas with her!") And why not? Weren't they always talking about how unhappy they were with their spouse? Didn't they tell their lover how wonderful it would be if the two of them could be together always?

And so the pressure mounts from both ends. As does the confusion about what's best to do. They feel troubled, lonely, and guilt-ridden. They feel like they're sitting on a powder keg that can blow their life to smithereens.

In fact, their emotions are all over the place.

CONFUSION. On the one hand, maybe they feel very hopeful about spending the rest of their life with their lover.

On the other hand, maybe it's starting to hit them how expensive getting a divorce will be. And not just financially. Emotionally and socially, as well.

And on the third hand, every time they think of getting back with their spouse, something happens and that relationship deteriorates, and they wonder, why bother?

On the fourth hand, every time they think about their kids—if they have kids—they start feeling guilty about what a divorce will do to those young and fragile psyches. And both men and women start being afraid that if they are not in their kids' lives as much, they'll lose their love. Their kids will think of them as the bad parent. And if their kids forget that for a moment, their ex will remind them.

And so the pressure and confusion deepen.

Feeling overwhelmed the way they do, maybe things aren't as great with their lover as they'd been, and they start wondering what's the point of staying in this new relationship. Or maybe they go the other way and feel much more pressure to end the marriage and so end the stress.

And if their spouse finds out, very soon a harrowing struggle gets going.

A THREE-WAY TUG-OF-WAR. There's so much suspicion and anger once an affair is revealed that it quickly becomes a three-way tug-of-war.

Let's say Alan is married to Betty (with whom he has two children) and is having an affair with Carol. Carol is going to push as hard as she can to get Alan to leave Betty, while trying not to push so hard that she pisses Alan off.

Betty is scared, and she is going to try to scare the crap out of Alan. She'll often push by threatening the most punitive divorce settlement she can think of. Either this will scare Alan into coming back to her, she thinks, or she will end up being well taken care of if he leaves her.

And Alan . . . well, Alan is genuinely confused about what's best to do, particularly because there are kids in the picture. And that makes him want to slow things down. But it's also in his interest to slow things down, because for the time being at least he's holding onto two relationships with two people, and he faces serious hurt if he loses or lets go of either one.

This is a recipe for a lot of stress and struggle, and it's also a recipe for things to stay up in the air for a surprisingly long time. Even though people want nothing more than to get things sorted out fast, the dynamics are in play for everyone to become paralyzed.

FEELING STUCK. No wonder so many people get into a curl-up-in-a-ball period, when they just don't know what's best to do. Things aren't wonderful in either relationship, and they can't figure out if it's them or the other person or the damned situation.

But still they hang in there, because they don't know what else to do, and they're afraid that whatever they do will just make things worse.

Of course, people often talk to a friend or a family member. These people may genuinely care, but they're rarely as helpful as hoped for. Friends and family are usually biased one way or another. What's more, people usually can't bring themselves to tell friends or family 100 percent of the story. Important considerations always get left out. And friends and family are rarely the best advisers.

IT ALL BLOWS UP. So people hang in there for as long as they can, until they get a big old wake-up call. Maybe it's an ulcer. Maybe it's a series of anxiety attacks, or even a heart attack. Maybe one of their kids starts acting out in school.

Maybe their boss reads them the riot act because he can tell that they're just not performing up to par. It's hard to concentrate at work, and for most people in this situation, job performance falls off, sometimes severely, putting their career at risk.

After all, carrying around a stressful problem like an affair takes a big toll. People get depressed. They lose sleep. Being in two relationships drains emotional energy, so they find it hard to give to the people they care about, and all their relationships suffer. Most people say that it's a heart-wrenching, confusing nightmare. It's like trying to juggle chainsaws when you don't know how to juggle.

Eventually they realize that the cost of what they're doing is unbearable.

Through it all, they're haunted by the most important question: "What do I want? What do I really, really want?"

"I JUST WANT WHAT'S BEST FOR EVERYONE"

The first answer that comes to mind for them is a heartfelt vision of personal happiness.

For one person it could be "If only we could heal the hurts from the past, and if only we could stop making each other mad the way we've done for so long now, and if only I could be forgiven for this affair, I'd want to go back to my partner."

For another person it could be "If only it wouldn't have a devastating effect on my kids, and if only it wouldn't take me away from my kids, and if only it wouldn't send me to the poorhouse, and if only I didn't feel so damned guilty, I'd want to divorce my spouse and be with my lover."

The choice would be a lot easier if it weren't for those damned "if onlys." But they're so real. And so confusing.

That's why, in the end, when people ask themselves what they really want, they find themselves saying that they don't want anyone to get hurt. They'd like everyone to get their needs met. They just want what's best for everyone. And they mean it.

But then what? Besides "what's best for everyone," what do people really want? Who do they want to be with? How do they want to make it happen? How do they find their way past the "if onlys," not dismissing them, but not being overwhelmed by them, either?

CHOOSE IT OR LOSE IT

One harmful way people deal with these questions grows out of feeling guilty. Because they feel guilty they feel they deserve to be punished. Because they feel they deserve to be punished they make bad decisions and do stupid things, and really do end up getting punished. Unfortunately, in the process they're not the only ones whose lives are ruined.

Another harmful way people deal with these questions is by doing nothing. In so many ways, doing nothing seems like the easiest, most attractive alternative. Hey, it's what they've been doing so far anyway. And it's been working.

But they're not stupid. The stress and anxiety they experience come from a good, commonsense place inside of them. They know that they're skating on thin ice, and that at any minute they could crash through. They're one errant e-mail, one untimely phone call, one careless credit card receipt away from disaster.

And so they know that the slogan "choose it or lose it" applies to them. Right now they have more freedom, more options, than they may ever have again. If they don't figure things out soon and start making the tough choices, then they may very well lose all the options they've been counting on. Spouse, lover, even children may stop wanting to have anything to do with them.

Here's a cautionary tale if there ever was one.

JOSH'S STORY

Josh, 40, had been married to Michelle, 38, for five years. They'd been pressured into getting married by Michelle's father, Dan, who owned the business Josh was working for. Josh convinced himself that he loved Michelle, and she was flattered that this really hand-some, dynamic guy wanted her.

But now their marriage had become a disappointment to both of them. It wasn't throwing dishes bad. Just blah. It was so clear that so much was missing that a couple of times they'd mentioned get-ting a divorce. Instead, Michelle got pregnant. All her hope and en-ergy went into the coming baby. Josh felt even more deflated.

Josh had been part of a running club and had often found him-self running next to Stacy, 29. They clearly liked each other. One day just the two of them showed up for a cross-country run. At one point Stacy twisted her ankle, and they sat in the woods and talked. A physical chemistry that had long been smoldering came roaring to life. They ended up making out like teenagers. It was more passion than Josh had felt in his entire relationship with Michelle.

RIDING THE TIGER. Within two weeks Josh and Stacy were having a full-blown affair. Motel rooms. New, hopefully secret e-mail accounts. A profound sense of yearning and romance.

For Josh it was awful. He was consumed by guilt and fear. If he got a divorce, especially if it was found out that he'd been cheating, his bright future with his father-in-law's business would be over. His dreams of a happy family with his new child would be over. At the same time, the thought of losing Stacy was horrible.

But it was also a relief. He had his nice little family life with Michelle. In fact, things there were better than ever. Michelle had been wondering at the miracle of how Josh suddenly managed to stop acting disappointed in her. She glowed in what looked like his sudden appreciation of her. And so she was more loving to him.

But Josh loved his relationship with Stacy just the way it was. As long as they could manage not to think about their future, as long as they could keep at bay Stacy's growing resentment at having to share him with Michelle, it was as if they'd entered this magical bubble of love every time they were together.

In spite of the negatives, Josh, like a heroin addict, kept wanting for things to go on the way they were.

Of course, when you're having an affair, just like when you're driving around on four bald tires, a blowout or worse is inevitable.

. . . OR WORSE. Stacy, unknown to Josh, was obsessed with soon turning thirty. It was great finding a man she loved, but the thought of turning thirty as some married guy's girlfriend, on the side, with no hope of ever being his wife, made her crazy. She started talking to some of her friends, and they all said she already was crazy. "These married guys never leave their wives, especially with a child on the way," they all said.

Stacy called Josh on the carpet about how hard it was for her to put up with playing second fiddle, with being a lady-in-waiting. She handed him what she thought was an ultimatum. Josh, thinking she was merely upset, said, "Look, I'm doing the best I can to get out of my marriage, but it's difficult. I have to play it very carefully. There's so much on the line now. Please be patient."

But Josh had lied about doing the best he could to get out of his marriage. Stacy knew he was lying. She could just tell. She dumped him on the spot in a way that was so final, it left Josh with no hope of ever working it out. He cried.

He went home to Michelle, brokenhearted but comforted that at least he still had his family. Unfortunately, in one of those ways life constantly imitates soap operas, Michelle was at home waiting to throw Josh out on his sorry ass.

THE WORST. It hadn't been just one thing. First there'd been that special blue, diamond necklace–size box she'd found in his inside raincoat pocket several days before her birthday. She'd been so excited. But her birthday came and went with nothing from Tiffany's. The next day, when she looked in his raincoat, the box had mysteriously disappeared.

Then, a few days later, Michelle was out walking their dachshunds when she ran into a friend, who said, "Oh, you know, I saw Josh the other evening at Riley's. I told him to say hi to you for me. Who was that woman he was with? She was gorgeous." *What woman?* Michelle wondered. There wasn't supposed to be any woman. *What night was that again? Wednesday? That was when Josh had said he had a meeting with a client.* But Josh was in the wholesale plumbing supply business. They don't have gorgeous women for clients.

Michelle was still hoping it was all a coincidence, but now they were very scary coincidences. So now she started snooping, with her heart pounding and a terrible, tight feeling in her throat. She tried to turn up incriminating e-mails on his computer, but she couldn't find anything.

Then she went through his drawers, and there in the midst of a pile of credit card statements she found some with entries for stays in a local motel.

Michelle sat on the bed, her mouth growing drier by the minute, and then she called the motel. She said she was Josh's bookkeeper, and she needed to verify these receipts. "Oh yes," the clerk said. "He was here on those days. It's right here in the computer. But I was on duty then, and I remember handing his wife the key card."

That was all Michelle needed to hear.

Within ten minutes of getting home that night, Josh's life as he'd known it was over.

. . .

Change the names, rearrange the genders, come up with different details, and stories like this happen all the time. And even if they don't turn out quite as catastrophically, the point is still the same: Choose it or lose it. The evidence is in. If people who are having an affair don't decide what they want to do, and how best to do it, sooner rather than later they will lose the freedom to decide.

TO TELL OR NOT TO TELL? Since we're talking about choose it or lose it, I want to answer a question a lot of people ask me. Should a person confess to their partner that they've had an affair?

No. Not even if you're asked point-blank.

Most people confess because they feel it will somehow discharge their guilt. But how does it make a person less guilty to inflict terrible pain on someone, which is what a confession will do? How does it make a person less guilty to put another person in a permanent state of hurt and grief and loss of trust and the inability to feel safe? How does it alleviate guilt to deal your relationship a potentially devastating blow?

A lot of people confess because they feel they "just have to be honest." Well, honesty is great. But it's a very abstract moral principle. A much more concrete, and much higher, moral principle is not hurting people. And when you confess to having an affair, you are hurting someone. More than you can imagine.

If you care that much about honesty, figure out who you want to be with, commit to that relationship, and devote the rest of your life to making it the most honest relationship you can. But confessing your affair is the kind of honesty that's unnecessarily destructive.

There are two huge exceptions to not telling. If you're having an affair *and you haven't practiced safe sex, even if it's only one time,* you *have* to tell. Again, the principle is minimizing hurt. But this time the greatest risk of hurt comes from inflicting a sexually transmitted disease, and relationships rarely recover from that.

You also have to tell if discovery is imminent or likely. If it's clear that you're going to be found out, then it's better for you to be the one to make the confession first.

I didn't always feel this way. But years of experience have taught me, someone who worships the truth, that this is one area in which the truth usually creates far more damage in the long run.

ASKING FOR DIRECTIONS

Choose it or lose it means people need to figure out what's best for everyone before they're found out. That gives them the greatest chance of healing the relationship if they decide to stay in it.

The problem is, how in the world can they figure out what to do?

Eventually, people who are having affairs find themselves caught in a strange dynamic. Periods of doing nothing alternate with periods of frantically trying to figure out what's best to do. Sometimes people find themselves wanting to be with whomever they're with at the moment. Sometimes they find themselves wanting to be with whomever they're *not* with at the moment.

Sometimes what seems best is totally controlled by the very last thing that happens to tug at their heartstrings. One day their child, heading off to school the way she does every morning, turns and says, "Bye, see you later," in a way that pierces them to the heart and makes them decide on the spot to stay in the marriage. Another day, sitting in the car in traffic, the rain coming down, the windshield wipers barely keeping up, they'll suddenly feel a surge of such loneliness that it becomes crystal clear that the only way they'll be happy is to be with their lover.

In these figuring-out periods, they'll talk to friends. But friends typically give conflicting advice.

And so they go, frantically looking for answers. Eventually, exhausted by this, they collapse back into doing nothing. And then back and forth the pendulum swings, from nothingness to panic, from panic to nothingness.

But in all of that, there are no answers.

So where *do* the answers lie?

REGRET-PROOFING THE FUTURE

Up until now I've been talking about "good people who have affairs." But if you're one of those people, then I've been talking about *you*. And for you the answers lie in learning from other people's experiences how to regret-proof every next step you take.

Not knowing how to do something isn't what makes someone stupid. Stupid is when you *won't* benefit from other people's experiences. When you *can't* benefit from someone else's experiences, then that's different. And that's where you've been until now.

But I can be the mentor or midwife or guide (pick your metaphor!) that you've been needing. Not because I'm so great but because I've walked through every inch of these dark woods with countless people who've lost their way like you, and I've learned how to shepherd them to safety. I've learned all the pitfalls and places where people get stuck. And I've learned how you can find your way out, to the best possible outcome, no matter how lost you may feel at the moment.

What holds it all together is the idea that you're regret-proofing every step you take. This is a new idea for many of us. We tend to look for what's "right" or what's "best." But when things are murky, the only solution is to take things one step at a time, and make sure that with each step you ask yourself what you can do that's least likely to lead to regret. Then things are most likely to turn out okay.

The old view of affairs is that they end up like a car crash, with the cut and bleeding survivors crawling out of the shattered windows. And sometimes it does feel like that. But it doesn't have to.

If you can learn from the experience of others and see how to regret-proof every step you take, you can end up with your life being renewed and with all the love you've been looking for.

Yes, you might ask, but where do I start?

Let me show you.

FIRST LEVEL

GETTING BEYOND GUILT

[2]

"I'M SO TIRED OF FEELING ASHAMED"

Well, you went ahead and got yourself into a real pickle, didn't you? No wonder you might find yourself jealous of those cool, calculating characters who don't care who they hurt. That would make things a lot easier—not being burdened by a guilt so thick and heavy that it paralyzes you and makes you stupid.

So what's the truth? I've already said that most men and women who have affairs are good people. But what's *your* opinion? Do you think you're a bad person, just because you're involved in two relationships? Not sure? Well, here's a test case. You tell me. Is Abby a bad person?

ABBY'S STORY

A couple of weeks after she started seeing me, Abby, 43, suddenly burst into tears. "I've been having an affair," Abby blurted out, sobbing. "I just couldn't tell you before. I was too ashamed. But I've been seeing a man off and on for five years now."

Abby felt terribly guilty. But before you judge her, look at the whole picture.

Abby would do anything for her seven-year-old son. She goes to church, too, and asks God to show her what she should do about the mess she's gotten herself into.

The fact is that years ago her marriage went south on her. Her husband, Mike, is cold and demanding and has a terrible temper—he's never hit Abby, but he's punched holes in the wall, and generally kept her in a state of anxiety. He's not a great lover. He's not a great dad, either. (This last one isn't just Abby's opinion. Everyone says that he's a real jerk with his son.)

It was his being a lousy husband that made Abby think of leaving. But it was his being a lousy father that made Abby feel trapped into staying. She wanted to be there to mitigate the damage he could do.

Who knows if it was fate or coincidence or what, but just when it was starting to become clear to Abby that her husband could never make her happy, she met Tom. Tom seemed to be everything Mike wasn't. Most of all, he kept being nice to Abby. For a woman like her, someone hungry for love and romance, there's nothing more seductive than a man who genuinely likes you. Like an accident looking for a place to happen, the next thing Abby knew she was having a full-blown affair with Tom.

ROSES AND FIREWORKS. In the little time they could find to be together, it was all roses and fireworks. But Abby was afraid of things getting out of control, and so she'd put off seeing Tom for months at a time in the hope that she'd forget him, or that her life with Mike would somehow change. Eventually she and Tom settled into a routine of getting together every six months for an afternoon of sex and romance in a nice downtown hotel.

Tom was married, too. (People often have an affair with some-one who is also in a committed relationship—simply because once they're out of their twenties, so many people are in committed rela-tionships.) His wife wasn't as bad as Mike, it's just that they no longer had anything in common. Their marriage was cold and dead. Tom would've divorced her in a minute.

What to do? Abby knew that for the sake of her son she could tough it out with her husband if she had to. But the thought of waiting until her son went off to college before she, by that time menopausal, could find love was devastating.

There was a way out. Abby was sure that if she begged Tom to leave his wife, and if she guaranteed that she'd leave her hus-band, then Tom would do it. They'd have a chance at happiness together. Tom was the one man she'd ever really loved, or who'd ever really loved her. But she was riddled with fear and guilt. Yes, she thought, Tom would do it, but would he be so crippled with guilt himself that it would curdle their love like orange juice poured into milk?

Besides, Abby worried, was their love real? Yes, of course, it felt like the most real thing in the world during that one special after-noon every six months, and during their rare, supersecret e-mails filled with yearning for each other. But all that was so romantic. She knew that Tom was a busy, driven, self-absorbed businessman. How could Abby feel confident that their chemistry was real and not the by-product of their hopes and needs and fantasies?

And if Abby married Tom, what would this do to her son, a sen-sitive boy who would then be coparented by a vengeful father?

Overwhelming as all this was, Abby had no one to talk to. She might have risked telling her sister, Beth. But there was a good chance Beth would tell her husband, and Abby couldn't risk that be-cause Beth's husband was good friends with Mike.

So Abby felt like a woman trapped in a minefield—whichever way she stepped there was risk of devastation.

So what's your verdict? Do you think Abby is a bad person? This is important because, in a way, it's your verdict on yourself.

DOING THE BEST YOU CAN

Abby never wanted to hurt anyone, and she did her best to avoid hurting anyone. At every step she was doing the best she could do. I don't see any other way of looking at her: She's a *good* person, of course.

And if you can say the same kinds of things about yourself, why wouldn't you say you're a good person, too? I'd have to say that you probably are, if you're like almost all the people I've worked with.

What about Abby getting involved with Tom in the first place? Of course cheating on your spouse isn't a moral act. I'm not claiming it is. But Abby was starved for love; that certainly makes her mistake understandable.

Some people in this situation *are* coldhearted users. They're in a perfectly good relationship, but if they think they can get away with a little action on the side, then, hey, why not go for it? And if their partner gets hurt, well, he or she should just get over it, they think.

Most good people who have affairs live in a very different reality. They never planned for it to happen. All they wanted was their share of the love and happiness that people can find in this life. But there was something missing, maybe a lot missing, in their relationship. Then they met someone, and the next thing you know, they're in two relationships, their love life is a mess, and they feel like they're going crazy.

Just to be sure about yourself, answer these questions honestly:

1. In general, do you feel guilty or worried about hurting the people in your life?
2. When it comes to your affair, do you constantly struggle

to come up with a resolution to the situation that would
be best for everybody?

3. Do you just want to find your share of love and happiness, and do you hope everyone else does, too?

If you answered *yes* to all three of these questions, then you can feel
confident that you're a good person.

You have good intentions. That's what's so frustrating. You know
you're at serious risk of making a mess. That's why you're afraid you
are a bad person. That's why you feel guilty and ashamed. But you
shouldn't feel that way. And I'll tell you why.

WHY YOUR GUILT IS NOT HELPING YOU NOW

It's not about letting you off the hook. If anything, I want to put
you *on* the hook, but only to help you move forward and clarify
things as fast as possible. The real reason you need to be relieved of
the sense of guilt and shame is that it's paralyzing. It makes you stupid. It leads you to make bad decisions.

Here's how this works. Guilt and shame are painful. And like
any form of pain, they absorb an enormous amount of energy and
attention. Before you know it, your top priority is to do whatever
you can to minimize your guilt and shame. This provokes you into
making impulsive moves. What's more, since guilt and shame are
making it hard for you to talk to people about your situation,
you're all alone with your feelings and don't have any wise confi-
dants.

And where does that put you? It means that you're very vulnerable to flying off in one direction or another, not because it's best
for you, not because it's best for anyone, but because you just can't
stand the guilt and shame anymore.

That's where Abby was when she first came to work with me.

One day she said, "I just can't do it to my son. He's such a sensitive kid. I don't want him to grow up the child of divorce." Anything to make the pain of guilt and shame go away.

But was this wise? Was this what was best for everyone? Maybe. But maybe not.

A couple of weeks later Abby said, "I just want to be with Tom. I miss him so much. I can't stand the hell I've been living in." And she was ready to walk out of her house and her marriage, taking her son with her, hoping for the best.

But as we talked about it, it became very clear that this sudden desire to fly into Tom's arms was mostly because she couldn't stand the emotional pain she'd been living with.

Being whipsawed by guilt and shame was not helpful. Abby came to see what she was really trying to accomplish. She wanted to find love. She wanted to take care of her son. She wanted to avoid hurting anyone. She didn't even want to hurt her husband, Mike. As a spiritual person she couldn't shake the thought that infidelity was a sin. But she also came to recognize that her good intentions and her struggle to figure out what was best to do qualified her as a good person.

And that freed Abby up. We worked out a plan. Her relationships with Mike and with Tom were two completely separate things. Abby came to see that if she stayed with Mike, she'd be condemning her son to grow up in a daily nightmare of anger and bitterness. That couldn't be good for anyone. And she'd be destroying any chance she had for happiness. So she decided to leave.

But Tom was another issue. She wasn't getting a divorce to be with Tom. She was getting a divorce because it was best for everyone. She's now in the process of discovering her relationship with Tom in a new light, free—at her end anyway—of the romantic haze of forbidden love.

But she's glad the rosy glow is gone. Now she has a chance to see Tom for who he really is. And that makes her feel confident that whatever she decides about Tom, she won't make a mistake.

LETTING GO OF GUILT

So take a deep breath, and when you exhale let go of all the guilt you've been feeling. Just say to yourself over and over "I may have made some mistakes, but I have good intentions, and that makes me a good person." Then keep a resolute focus on just what your intentions are—to find love and have a good life without hurting anyone unduly. Focusing on your intentions will help you realize them.

And that will take you very far toward making sure the path you're taking is free of regrets. If at each fork in the road you take the path that's least likely to lead to regret, you'll do just fine.

BELOW THE SURFACE

Your situation may be different from Abby's. You may be a man, not a woman. You may be single. You may not have kids. You may be gay. You may be a lot younger, or older.

But below the surface there are strong threads that connect your situation to that of everyone who's in relationships with two people. You all need the same things: help and hope.

That's what Abby got. You can get that, too. And you will. That's what the rest of this book is for.

The most important thing for you to have in mind now is that you're in this situation because you're trying to make your life better and do what's best for everyone. That's your real goal, and you can accomplish it. In fact, you're already starting to accomplish it.

And that's why you can stop feeling guilty and start feeling more like the good person you really are.

But I think there's something else you need that will help you move forward. You need to understand how a smart, good person like you got into this situation in the first place. As you'll see, maybe you knew what you were doing all along. That's what we'll deal with when we get to the next level.

UNCOVERING THE TRUE MOTIVES

3

THE SEVENTEEN DIFFERENT
KINDS OF AFFAIRS

You can't know what to do about your affair until you know why you're in it in the first place. The reasons you got into the affair will point you toward where you need to go now. How can you tell why you got into your affair? You just have to know what kind of affair it is. Each kind has its own motivation. Each kind points to its own resolution. Let's take this a step at a time.

CRAZY LIKE A FOX

People who are having an affair usually find themselves caught in the following knot:

> I'm in a confusing mess.
> So now I have to think hard and figure out what to do.
> But *I* got myself into this confusing mess.

So why should I trust myself or listen to myself for advice?
So I must be the kind of person who'd get themselves into
a confusing mess.
So there's probably no point in trying to do anything about
this mess.

There you have it. This is why good people who get involved in two relationships usually have such difficulty trusting themselves. And that's a problem. It's not just paralyzing; it's also not well founded. Maybe you made your own love life go haywire, but you have often been a source of great wisdom and help to your friends who are facing similar issues.

You need to start feeling that you can trust yourself. So if you're in two relationships, here's what I have to say to you: I know you feel like a complete idiot, both because you got into this situation and because it's so hard for you to figure out how to get out of it. What's more, I know you feel there's something fundamentally wrong with you. Only someone who is bent in the wrong direction would have done what you did, you think. *But there's probably nothing wrong with you. In fact, you're probably much smarter than you think.*

You might be surprised to hear me say that. There are some really screwed-up people out there, and we all have moments when we're blind and impulsive. But that's not usually dominant. Instead, what I see is that we're smarter and more oriented toward health and growth than we seem.

An interviewer once asked me if I could sum up everything I know about psychology in ten words or less. I said, "Hell, I can do it in two words: People cope."

That means that you are able to cope, too. You are someone who has coped in the past and will cope in the future. And if you can accept this, in spite of your mistakes and blind spots, you will be a lot less anxious. And if you're less anxious, you will be in a much better position to figure out what you should do and how you should do it.

It's not just that you can cope in general. You are coping right now—there's a reason you're doing what you're doing. You want to know what that reason is? It's coming up in a minute. The point is that you've been having an affair as a way to cope. If you can see that, you're lucky. John had to go through hell to figure it out.

LESS ANXIETY, MORE CLARITY—WHAT A DEAL!

John, 36, came to see me with the emotional equivalent of a toothache. He was a much loved veterinarian, a sweet man, someone with a healing heart. But he was also someone in a souring marriage. His wife was a good person, but they'd long ago run out of things to talk about. And for reasons John couldn't understand, in the past few years his wife had become increasingly critical of him.

John couldn't figure out if they were distant because they were fighting or fighting because of their growing distance. It seemed as though his wife was changing, but John couldn't shake the suspicion that he was the one who'd been withdrawing from her. All he knew for sure was that, as the distance grew, the tension grew, and the sniping grew. It now felt like one of those marriages held together only by children and habit.

That's when a very vulnerable John met Patty. She was a divorced teacher who lived in their neighborhood—they met while walking their dogs around a local pond. Their relationship started out casual and fun, soon turned affectionate, and before long became sexual. It wasn't a passionate affair; it was all about comfort and companionship.

THE TRUTH COMES OUT. John both loved and hated every minute of the affair. Part of his relationship with Patty was great. She could be fun, warm, and loving, all stuff missing from his marriage. There's nothing better than falling in love with someone. It was made even better because of the way Patty understood his bruised and hungry heart and found a way to heal it.

At the same time, he was amazed to see how quickly Patty's tiresome traits showed themselves. She could be very self-involved and bossy, and she sometimes had an uncomfortable way of giving lectures about the obvious. John felt it was just a matter of time before she, too, would start being critical of him.

Mostly there was the good stuff, though. The bad stuff passed like a rain squall on a sunny day. For now, he couldn't get enough of Patty. But John sensed that over the horizon many storms were waiting for him.

One day Patty kept calling John at work, and they had a series of tense, unhappy conversations. He'd been hoping that they'd be able to find a couple of stolen hours during the long weekend coming up, but family plans had nixed that. Patty was upset. Why couldn't he find more time for her? Why wasn't he trying harder? How could she know that he wasn't just using her?

The questions kept coming. Was he still sleeping with his wife? John tried to weasel out of answering this last one. But Patty's response was basically that he was lying if he said no and betraying her if he said yes.

He was in so much pain after those calls. That night after his wife went to bed—she was a deep sleeper and a loud snorer—John snuck out of the house. He found himself lurking in front of Patty's house in the hope that for some crazy reason Patty would take it into her head to walk outside at one o'clock in the morning only to find . . . him. Then, maybe, somehow, they would fall into each other's arms.

That's when John knew he was in big trouble. He was starting to act like a crazy man.

PUTTING THE GENIE BACK IN THE BOTTLE.
Lurking outside his lover's house in the middle of the night
sobered John up and cleared his vision. Somehow he was able to
see past their present passion. It hit him that Patty was just another
woman, and that soon their great love affair would turn into just
another relationship. Nothing special, in other words, nothing
worth breaking up a family over. He wasn't experiencing the wonderfulness of Patty, just the wonderfulness of the first stages of an
affair.

He'd been telling her that he liked the music she liked, but he
really didn't. And it wasn't just the music.

At the same time, John's affair showed him his marriage in a different light. He compared how he treated Patty with how he
treated his wife. What a difference. Why *wouldn't* his wife turn sour,
given the way he'd been treating her? Why *wouldn't* she treat him
the way Patty had if he had been treating her the way he treated
Patty?

John had what amounted to a revelation. He hadn't been a man
trapped in a bad marriage who was being rescued by some angel.
No. He was a man who'd probably done more than his share to
sour his marriage, and who had found it easier to find love with another woman with whom he had no history.

It was still confusing, but through the confusion John saw that
he'd had his fling, and that it was bringing him back to his wife. And
it was true: He was better able to appreciate her and more willing
to work on their marriage. He felt he had no choice. With tears, and
in spite of pangs of misgiving, John ended his affair.

His wife never found out about the affair. As time passed, whenever his mind went back to Patty, John couldn't help thinking that
the whole experience had been a terrible waste.

But had it?

HIDDEN WISDOM

John's story is an instance of what I call hidden wisdom. I see it with almost everyone who gets involved with two people. Underlying the complicated mess is a kind of deep and delicate wisdom that, if listened to and followed carefully, leads to the healing *that was the point of getting into this mess in the first place.*

The outcome is different for everybody. Some people, like John, find their way back to their spouse. Some choose to be with their lover. And some find their way to get free and clear of all entanglements, so they can start with a fresh slate.

In all of these cases the hidden wisdom lay in someone having an experience that blew away a fog that had settled on their life and showed them who they really were and what they really needed to do.

Think of it as a kind of radical but necessary medical procedure. John was in a marriage in cardiac arrest. What he needed was a kind of defibrillator. Patty turned out to be that defibrillator.

TWO AFFAIRS IN ONE

My research and clinical experience have shown me that there are seventeen different kinds of affairs. What kind did John have?

In part, John got involved in a *see-if* affair. Sometimes you can sink so deep into the depths of a relationship that you have no idea what you're missing, or if you're missing anything at all. And yet you sense that something is missing, and you want to see if you can find it elsewhere. Maybe something sexual, maybe something emotional, maybe something else.

Patty was John's way of *seeing if* the grass was greener on the other side. Well, it was certainly green. And it was refreshing. But it wasn't green*er*.

It was also a *surrogate-therapy* affair. This is a clumsy and dangerous kind of therapy that can easily kill a relationship. But, hey, I'm not saying that you are a genius who knows exactly what you're doing. I'm just saying that your wisdom lies in sensing that there's something amiss, and in doing something radical that, *if handled just right,* will give you clarity or help you make a much needed move.

John's affair was therapeutic because it woke him up from his helplessness and inertia. It gave him the kind of energy he needed, in turn, to wake up his marriage. It also gave him the insights he needed to see his part in his marriage's bad state.

I don't know what kind of affair yours has been. There are seventeen possibilities, so yours might very well be different from John's. The point is that there *is* a hidden wisdom in what you are doing. The kind of affair you're having is an expression of that wisdom.

That's ultimately where your hope can come from. You'll soon see what you were doing to try to heal your life (yes, in a very dangerous way, but we can make it less dangerous). And you *can* heal it.

THE REASON FOR YOUR AFFAIR

Here's the real reason good people have affairs: You're in a relationship that has some problems. You don't know how to fix those problems, although you've probably tried. You're frustrated and confused. You don't know what to do. You don't even know how to think about what's going on. What you need are two things: information and change. And sometimes an affair is the best way to get those things.

I don't want you to misunderstand me. I'm not encouraging

affairs. Along with the hidden wisdom comes some very obvious stupidity. People can and do ruin their lives by getting involved in two relationships. But you are where you are right now. And there's still wisdom in what you're doing, and we need to respect that.

I find that people can best recognize their own motives by looking at the various kinds of affairs. When you see yours, you'll recognize it.

This is important, because your reason for being in those two relationships points to what you really want to get out of your life. And it's only when you understand *that* that you have a chance of resolving your love life. When you know the kind of affair you're having, you know what you're trying to get for yourself.

So here, then, are the seventeen most common kinds of affairs:

1. see-if affair
2. ejector-seat affair
3. heating-up-your-marriage affair
4. distraction affair
5. break-out-into-selfhood affair
6. I-just-needed-to-indulge-myself affair
7. let's-kill-this-relationship-and-see-if-it-comes-back-to-life affair
8. unmet-needs affair
9. having-experiences-I-missed-out-on affair
10. do-I-still-have-it? affair
11. surrogate-therapy affair
12. trading-up affair
13. accidental affair
14. revenge affair
15. midlife-crisis affair
16. sexual-panic affair
17. midmarriage-crisis affair

As you see which ones apply to you, you'll begin to see what to do.

Please note: Affairs usually serve more than one purpose at a time, so even if you identify with one type, keep on reading. More than one type of affair will probably apply to you. After all, you're a complicated person!

THE SEE-IF AFFAIR. In this kind of affair, the real reason people are in a second relationship is to *see if* being with a new person will solve their problems. In its purest form, it's sincere, if unconscious, research.

What are they researching? It might be that they've been in a relationship for a long time, things have frayed, and they just want to see if they can do better.

It might be that they're in a fairly new relationship, and they suddenly realize how little experience they've had. What if they could've done a lot better? They'd like to see if that's true.

It might be that they've changed, or their partner's changed, in some important ways. Now they'd like to see if they fit much better with someone else.

It might be that something is missing in their relationship—sex, conversation, fun, an emotional connection, anything essential for their sense of satisfaction. They want to see if it makes much of a difference if they get it with someone else.

You can understand right away how this type of see-if affair can help. In every case there's a kind of hidden wisdom guiding people to discover a truth about their marriage and themselves.

Remember what happened with John. Ultimately, it *strengthened* his marriage when he went to see if the grass was greener on the other side and found that it wasn't. *It's often better to find out and be done with it than to endlessly yearn and speculate.* Like John, sometimes we just don't know how good we have it until we have something else to compare our relationship to.

Of course, John's story ended up with him going back to his wife. But for other people the story can end in other ways. Someone might have an affair to see if things can be better with a new person and come back with the answer "Hell, yes."

Does this apply to you? Take a moment to reflect:

> If you're honest with yourself, would you say that you've been using your second relationship to shed light on your first?

Let me illustrate. Let's say you and your partner don't have all that much in common. Is it possible, then, that you got involved with this other person, with whom you do have something in common, to see if that makes as big a difference as you thought it might?

Or, suppose sex with your partner has gotten all too routine, and sex is important to you. Is it possible that you've been monitoring the course of your sexual relationship with the other person to see if that gets routine, too, because if it does, then that might change the way you feel. After all, if you discover that in your experience sex always ends up becoming routine, then you might realize that your partner is the person you want to have routine sex with for the rest of your life.

That's the pattern of a see-if affair: Whether you realized it going in or not, you were conducting an investigation.

What does this mean for you? Take what you're doing seriously. You're in this affair because you really do need to find something out for yourself. So don't let your feelings for the other person carry you away too much. Instead, answer the question that your affair is asking: What are you trying to *see if*?

Suppose you realize that you're trying to see if you can be happier with someone else. Well, *are* you happier? Suppose you wanted to see if you could be more sexually fulfilled. Well, *is* the sex actually better, and does that make the relationship better? That was what you wanted to know.

If you're not happier, then you know that you don't need to be in that second relationship. It's served its purpose. If you are happier . . . after all, that's what you wanted to find out.

THE EJECTOR-SEAT AFFAIR. Any time you have an affair there's the danger that it will blow your marriage out of the water. Most people don't want that. They'd like to be able to decide whether they want to stay or not.

But some people feel trapped in their primary relationship.

It could be inertia—they're not happy, but they know that they're not the kind of person to initiate a breakup.

It could be comfort—they know that things are too good for them to ever leave on their own.

It could be guilt—they can't deal with the emotional burden of hurting the other person by breaking up with them.

It could be pressure from friends and family—everyone's created this image of this couple as the perfect couple, and they're reluctant to disappoint everybody.

An ejector-seat affair is a way of getting out of a trap.

Does this apply to you?

How would you feel if your partner found out about your affair? Would you be relieved?

Maybe it's hard for you to admit this. If so, ask yourself this:

Have you been careless about getting caught? Have you accidentally left clues lying around?

To confirm that this kind of affair applies to you, ask yourself this:

Would you say that you have an unhappy primary relationship that you feel trapped in?

Yes answers point to an ejector-seat affair.

What does this mean for you? Sometimes an affair really is the jolt that's needed to end a relationship. You need to accept the wisdom that led you to this. Stop being in denial about how unhappy you've been and how trapped you've felt in this relationship. Accept the fact that you know what you're doing. And now get on with it. You're not doing anyone any favors by holding on to a relationship that's broken beyond your desire to fix it.

But don't turn your ejector-seat affair into more than it is. If it is a way to get out of your relationship, that doesn't necessarily mean you should make a commitment to the person you are having the affair with. Don't let the very guilt or inertia that was trapping you in your primary relationship get you stuck in this new relationship. It's only a good relationship for you if it's a good relationship, and you may need to take time to see if that's true.

THE HEATING-UP-YOUR-MARRIAGE AFFAIR. The effect this type of affair may have on a marriage can be surprising as this is not the way most people think things work. And it's not the way things work most of the time. But it is the way things work *some* of the time. Surprisingly often, in fact.

Here's the classic scenario. You have an affair. It's not about being madly in love with someone. In fact, it's strangely lackluster. Your partner finds out. He or she is really upset, mad, devastated, all those bad things. But at the same time, amazingly, things get a lot hotter in bed. This happens more often than you might think.

I've heard colleagues offer a dozen reasons for why this is so: competition; kinkiness; fear; the need for something, anything, to spice things up—these are all possible reasons. But whatever the reason, there's something about you being caught in an affair that wakes up your spouse sexually and maybe even romantically.

Does this apply to you? Just two questions:

Is your lover someone you're not having a great love affair with?
Has your spouse found out about your affair, and has it made your spouse more sexual with you?

Yes and *yes*? That's all you need to know to see if this applies to you.

What does this mean for you? In most cases that I've seen, this affair dies a natural death, and the marriage gets better. The heating up of marital sex is a sign that there was something there that needed shaking up.

But you're not out of the woods yet. The aftermath has to be handled sensitively. Your primary relationship has to be healed. You'll find everything you need to do this later in this book when we get to the sixth level: Healing the Past, Building a Future.

THE DISTRACTION AFFAIR. People have a way of displacing their needs and their energy from one thing onto another. Instead of doing what they need to do, because that's too difficult or scary, they do what they can do. They have an affair to distract themselves.

For example, Helena, 41, after a successful career in advertising, found herself stuck at home with two little kids and a bad mood. This was the life she'd thought she wanted, but now she realized she didn't like it. Of course she loved her kids madly. But like many women, she felt the walls closing in. She knew she needed to do something with her life, and staying home wasn't it. But she didn't want to go back to working in an ad agency. That experience had taught her that she was talented and imaginative, but it had also shown her that she didn't want to stay in advertising.

Feeling lost on top of feeling trapped, feeling hungry for a new life but not knowing what that was or how to get it, was a real crisis for Helena. It made her miserable. So, to make a long story short, she had an affair. Of course it didn't feel like a distraction. It felt fun and exciting and stimulating. She felt as though she was getting what she wanted from a new life. But it wasn't a new life. It wasn't even love, Helena realized when she was honest with herself. It was just a distraction.

The details might vary but this is how distraction affairs work. You can't get what you need, and you don't know how to get what you need, so you get involved with someone else.

But even here, there may be a kind of hidden wisdom at work. It may be that you need to make some changes in your life but you're not ready to yet. The distraction affair can be a way of channeling your enormous energy and desire for change into a direction that, risky as it may be, is less dangerous than changing your life before you're ready.

Does this apply to you? Just two questions here:

Looking back carefully at what things were like before your affair, would you say that you were more unhappy about how your life was going than about your relationship?

Did you feel stuck in your life but didn't know what to do about it?

Yes answers to both of these questions are a sign that you're having a distraction affair.

What does this mean for you? If you're in a distraction affair, you're in tremendous jeopardy. Not only do you risk ending a perfectly good relationship, but the pain and craziness of struggling and breaking up might just delay even further doing what you really need to do, which is figuring out how you want to live. This means facing some short-term pain for some long-term gain. You need to end the affair, nice as it is, save your relationship, and do the hard work of figuring out what to do with yourself.

THE BREAK-OUT-INTO-SELFHOOD AFFAIR. In a way, this is the opposite of the distraction affair. With this affair you're finding your way back to who you really are and what's most important to you. It's as if part of you were lost and something about the affair helps you find the missing piece.

Martin, 32, had been in a committed relationship with Jim for seven years. The relationship was not great but okay. One thing that kept churning inside of Martin was the fact that his life with Jim was very materialistic. Jim was a hotshot lawyer. He was all about making as much money as possible and having the plushest lifestyle he could. This was intoxicating for Martin, because he'd grown up in a lower-middle-class household that had been dreary.

But Martin had wanted to be a poet. He'd even been published. All that had gotten lost with Jim. Then Martin met Carson. Carson was a professor of English literature who wrote a lot of reviews of contemporary fiction and poetry. Carson exemplified the world Martin felt he'd lost.

It was so exciting for Martin to reconnect not only with that world but with his own creative interests, which had been so stifled for so long. As Martin said about Carson, "He makes me feel more like the person I want to be—the person I forgot lived inside of me."

Fortunately, before it was too late, Martin had figured out what many people in this situation never realize. The affair meant so much to him not because being with Carson was better than being with Jim—it wasn't—but because it gave him back himself.

He ended things with Carson and committed to struggling with Jim to make changes in their life so he could get back the missing pieces of himself.

Many people aren't as lucky as Martin. They confuse the excitement of reclaiming themselves in the new relationship (which is what is really going on) with truly being a good fit with the other person. They end a perfectly good primary relationship that could have accommodated their true self more easily than they'd thought.

Does this apply to you? Come on now, tell the truth:

> Is what's best about this affair the fact that you're getting in touch with some part of yourself that you've been afraid was lost?

> If so, then you know what your affair is about.

What does this mean for you? If you're in a break-out-into-selfhood affair, then accept it for what it is. It's not the affair itself that you need; you can let that go before it destroys your life. What you need is a way to bring back into your life some important missing part of you. Clearly that's been difficult, but you need to fight for it before you give up on your primary relationship.

And what is it that you need to bring back into your life? Look at what was best about the affair, the part of it that made you really come alive. If it wasn't being with your lover while you happened to go sailing or horseback riding, but instead was the sailing or horseback riding while you happened to be with your lover, then you know what you need more of in your life.

But it might be something deeper. It might be something like getting in touch with your creative side (that's what happened for Martin). It might be being able to stand up for yourself. Or getting back in touch with how much you love being in the country. Whatever it is, it's something that has made you happy in the affair that was different from just being with the other person.

You've just shown yourself that getting it is so important to you that you're willing to risk hurting the people you care about. If it's that important to you, then you need to do something about it. But it doesn't necessarily mean that you need to end your primary relationship.

THE I-JUST-NEEDED-TO-INDULGE-MYSELF AFFAIR. This sounds pretty bad, doesn't it—cheating on your partner just to give yourself a treat? But it's more common than you think, and maybe more understandable. Thoreau said that people lead lives of quiet desperation. Some of us lead lives of married desperation.

Let's face it: These days, with all the stresses and sacrifices that relationships are filled with, many of us feel deprived. And then, if the relationship isn't working out so well, and there's a lot of anger, and no one has anything to give to anyone, the need to indulge yourself can be very strong. So strong that even people who wouldn't otherwise have an affair have one anyway. It's not noble, but it is understandable.

Does this apply to you? Imagine this scenario. You've been working very hard. You're not getting paid enough for what you do. Your boss isn't very complimentary or supportive. From the minute you get to work until the minute you leave the office, there's a lot of stress and frustration. One Thursday morning you wake up, and even though you hadn't planned this, even though you're not the kind of person who would ever do this, you call in sick. You're not sick; you just need a day off. And then since the next day is Friday, you take that day off, too.

It's a real indulgence, but it's one you very much needed. An indulgence affair feels a lot like this. They're rarely planned. In fact, they're rarely about the person you're having an affair with. Answer this:

> Although you feel guilty, do you also feel you deserve this affair, and do you enjoy how good it feels? And yet would you feel perfectly fine if the affair ended?

> If so, you know it's an indulgence affair.

What does this mean for you? If their affair is just an indulgence, people tend to feel even more guilty than if their affair is about falling in love, or if it's about how utterly barren and miserable their marriage is.

The danger with the indulgence affair is that guilty feelings play terrible tricks on people and lead them into big trouble. Trying not to feel guilty, they make a much bigger deal about the affair than they should. Sometimes they confess to their partner when they really should keep their mouths shut. Sometimes, out of guilt, they stay, even though they really should be getting out of the primary relationship (although they should probably not be getting permanently involved with their lover). Sometimes they make a disastrous commitment to someone they're having a transient relationship with.

But an indulgence affair is just that. Write it off as something you really needed. Figure out what's making things so unrewarding in your primary relationship, and do something about it. And find a way to manage your guilt. But don't turn a mistake into a disaster by making this kind of affair into a bigger deal than it is.

THE LET'S-KILL-THIS-RELATIONSHIP-AND-SEE-IF-IT-COMES-BACK-TO-LIFE AFFAIR. What happened to Tracy and Richard, both 29, is surprisingly common. For the previous three years their relationship had been very intense, difficult, but often rewarding. Lots of bad stuff, but lots of good stuff. So, of course, lots of drama. At one point Tracy and Richard went through a rough patch. There seemed to be more fights, fewer good times, and they both started feeling very discouraged about their relationship. It seemed all the more painful because of their memories of how wonderful it had been, even recently.

Then Tracy did something crazy and risky. She had an affair with someone at work. Interestingly, she didn't go to extraordinary lengths to keep it a secret, and before long Richard found out. In their case, as in most cases, the impact on their marriage was like giving poison to someone who is already sick. But wait a minute. Isn't that the way chemotherapy works, and isn't chemotherapy designed to *save* someone's life?

Which is it? Did Tracy want to kill her marriage or bring it back to life? The answer is, *both*. She wanted exactly what she did:

to deal her marriage a perhaps fatal blow, and then see what would happen.

In her blind, clumsy way, that's what Tracy's inner wisdom was really trying to do. Somehow she and Richard would be forced to grapple with each other, and the intensity of how they really felt would throw down the icy walls that had grown up between them. If it didn't kill their relationship, it would save it.

And that's exactly what happened. Richard found out about Tracy's affair. They had a huge fight. Richard punched a hole in their bedroom door and stormed out of the house. Surprisingly, though, over the next few days Richard and Tracy started missing each other. They talked on the phone. With tremendous feelings of guilt they both acknowledged how they'd let stupid things ruin a relationship that had so much good in it. And they both agreed that they couldn't bear to say good-bye to the good things they had—the great conversations, the great sex, the ability they had to laugh with each other. And they made a commitment to work at healing their relationship.

Tracy's affair didn't kill their relationship. It brought it back to life.

With this kind of affair, you never know how it will turn out. You just need to know one way or the other.

Does this apply to you? Richard and Tracy's scenario speaks for itself:

> Does it resonate for you?
> Can you identify with Tracy's need to know for sure whether their relationship was on or off?
> As another clue, is there something a little fishy about your affair—either it doesn't feel so great, or you're having it with someone who clearly isn't right for you?

These are the signs that you're having an affair to see if it kills your relationship or if your relationship can come back to life.

What does this mean for you? You've got to be very careful here. This is a risky experiment. You could destroy something very important to you. Bringing your relationship back to life by having an affair is like a total amateur trying to cure a cancer patient with chemotherapy. There are many more ways for this scenario to go wrong than for it to go right.

If you want to preserve the possibility of your relationship coming back to life, then you need to end your affair *yesterday*. You need to make a huge, showy, passionate plea to your spouse for the two of you to go into couples therapy, work on your relationship, restore all the good stuff that's been there, and clear away all the crap that's built up.

And then see what happens. You'll soon find out.

THE UNMET-NEEDS AFFAIR. We say it so casually: Nobody's perfect. And of course that's true. The problem is, there might be some way your partner isn't perfect that ends up with an important need of yours going unmet. Then what?

This is a profound dilemma. If you go outside the relationship to get that important need met, that can be seen as a betrayal. But if you end a good relationship to someone you love just to get some important need met, that seems like an awful waste.

For example, your partner might be wonderful in every respect except that he's not particularly interested in sex, or very good at it. If sex is very important to you, then suddenly you have a big unmet need. And this leads to lots of people getting involved in a second relationship to get the sex that they're not getting in their first.

Sex may be the unmet need that gets the most headlines, but unmet-needs affairs are just as often about something other than sex. In fact, the most common unmet need is for an emotional connection. But it could be for anything.

I once worked with a guy who was connected to the mob. As Tommy, 38, put it, "I guess you'd say I'm kind of an enforcer. Look, I done some bad things, Doc. But that's not what I want to talk about."

What he wanted to talk about were his relationships. Things had frayed in his marriage, but his biggest unmet need was for intelligent, informed conversation, something his bimbette of a wife evidently had little of. He got involved with another woman who taught high school civics and read *Time* every week. He bought a house for her a block and a half away from the house he shared with his wife. Sometimes he'd sleep in one house, sometimes the other.

Inevitably, the two women found out about each other. More surprisingly, they got together and jointly confronted him, something even this certified tough guy found intimidating. "You gotta choose, Tommy," his wife said. "It's either me or her."

"Yeah," his lover said.

"Gimme a week," Tommy said.

"You got two days," his wife said.

"Yeah," his lover said.

In the end he divorced his wife and married his lover, even though, he said, sex with his wife was better. Why did he? Because his lover was much more interesting for him to spend time with. "She's up on things," Tommy told me. "I like that."

Sometimes it's not until people have an affair that they can figure out how important some unmet need of theirs really is.

By the way, once I'd helped him with his relationship issues, Tommy wanted to stop therapy. "Well, you know, I can't make you come," I said, and in Tommy's case that was *definitely* true. "But I have to say that I'm very unhappy about the work you do. It's just wrong, and it's very dangerous for you."

"I know. I know. I'm working on it. I'm building up a little business. And once it really gets going, I'll stop the other stuff."

"What's your new business?" I asked.

"I'm an exterminator." There was a pause. I looked at him. "You know, bugs."

Sorry for the digression, but I thought you'd want to know.

Does this apply to you? Think about why you've been unhappy in your primary relationship:

> Would you say you focus more on who your partner is as a whole, or on some specific need of yours that's important and that your partner cannot or will not meet?

> Now think about your lover.

> Would you say that a major attraction for you is that your lover meets this need?

The more your affair seems to be about this particular unmet need, the more likely that it's an unmet-needs affair.

What does this mean for you? It's important to think through very carefully what you do about an unmet-needs affair.

The question is, what does this affair tell you about how important your unmet need really is to you?

Lots of times unmet needs seem important only because they're not being met. It's the craving, the deprivation, that makes them loom. Once the need is met you realize, oh, it's not as big a deal as I'd thought.

A woman I worked with had been somewhat unhappy in her marriage for years. And Susan, 37, connected her unhappiness with a need to have sex with a woman. The longer this need went unmet, the more it seemed like a big deal. Finally, one day she announced to me that she and a college friend had gotten together and "it" had happened.

"And?" I asked.

She sighed. "It was okay. But for me, I don't need to do that again. I thought it would be such a big deal. It's weird—I really am straight." And she laughed.

She never told her husband, but she started putting more energy into her marriage. Slowly the cloud that had been there for a long time lifted.

Once you've gotten an unmet need out of your system, it might not seem like such a big deal anymore. This is one of many reasons why affairs are so often transient. They only turn into devastating betrayals if they're revealed, and that's a tragedy if the whole reason for the affair was for it to serve as a kind of virus passing through your system, in the end leaving you back where you started.

Sometimes people "fall into" an affair, and that turns out to be their wake-up call. They realize that their unmet need is much more important to them than they'd thought. Okay, but that realization is a very different thing from what you ultimately should do about the affair.

Just because you're so happy that your unmet need is finally being met doesn't mean you should end your marriage. It just means that you need to take it more seriously. Going into couples therapy with your spouse to work on getting your need met might be a lot better than starting a new relationship where you'll find you have who-knows-what new unmet needs.

But sometimes there are unmet needs that are essential to our happiness. Suppose you're with someone who's a decent enough person but has no capacity for being affectionate to you. Or you're with someone who just can't manage to talk to you about anything that's really important to you (the way Tommy's wife was).

In cases like these, an affair can be an important way of confirming that yes, you do have a real need, and this need is very important to you, and satisfying it makes all the difference. And maybe that clearly points to the need to end your primary relationship.

But you have to be careful. *It doesn't necessarily mean that you need to be with the person you've been having an affair with.* Your affair was a learning experience, teaching you something important about your need. Fine. But don't let gratitude commit you to it unless it's a good relationship in more dimensions than just getting that specific need met.

THE HAVING-EXPERIENCES-I-MISSED-OUT-ON AFFAIR. This is a variation on the unmet-needs affair. This time, though, the unmet need isn't something in the present; it's something from the past that you missed out on. And there's a part of you that believes that to feel complete you have to have this experience.

Women often have affairs like this. Even today they sometimes come into relationships without a lot of experience. They have an affair to make sure they haven't missed out on something important.

There's a time when we're young that's just right for trying out experiences, even different selves. For example, what is it like to be with someone from a very different class or ethnic background? What is it like to be with someone much older, or younger? What is it like to be with someone who's very romantic or very cool or very rich or very artistic? What is it like to be with someone who just wants to throw you down on the bed and have sex with you all the time?

Does this apply to you? Affairs can be so exciting that it's hard to see them for what they are. If you remember the theme song to *The Love Boat*, it has the phrase "exciting and new." That's what affairs have going for them. All you can do is be painfully honest with yourself. Look at what you're getting out of the affair:

> **Aside from all the stuff that's exciting and new, what's the most important thing you're getting out of it?**

If it's something that you've missed out on, then you know that getting that missing experience is the point of the affair.

What does this mean for you? The issue is whether this affair is just an opportunity to take something off your to-do list or a way to reassess your whole marriage. Okay, fine, you always wanted to have a relationship with a really rich guy or with a woman with really big breasts. Now you have. You should be able to say that you've gotten it out of your system. It shouldn't change your life.

But what if the thing you missed out on was something you really need to be happy in a relationship? What if you missed out on being with someone who's, for example, nice to you? Or very romantic? Or interesting to talk to?

Be honest about how big a deal this is for you. Only then can you decide how big a threat this is to your relationship.

THE DO-I-STILL-HAVE-IT? AFFAIR. Both men and women report that problems in a relationship can damage their confidence and self-esteem. And so people sometimes have affairs whose real purpose is to prove something to themselves: They're still attractive; they're still able to be attracted to someone; they're still good people; they still feel sexual desire; they can still have lots of fun, or be a good lover.

Affairs like these become more common as we hit middle age. But even a young mother can be seriously affected by wondering if she still has it.

Does this apply to you? Just answer one question:

What do you find is really gratifying to you about this affair?

If you can honestly say that it's more about feeling better about yourself than feeling good about being with the other person, it might be the do-I-still-have-it? affair that you're going through.

What does this mean for you? Surprisingly often, affairs like these renew the primary relationship. At least, it works that way if people can contain the damage.

After all, you wanted to find out if you still have it, and you found that you *do* still have it, so now you can take your newfound confidence back into your primary relationship and the two of you can benefit from it.

With affairs like these it's usually very worthwhile to examine closely what it is about your relationship that was making you feel that you don't have it. This is where you can learn the most about whether to stay in or get out of this relationship.

If your partner is someone who's undermining your self-confidence, that's very serious and needs to be addressed directly. If this can't be remedied, it might mean you need to end your marriage.

THE SURROGATE-THERAPY AFFAIR. Therapists perform an important role in our society. Their most important function is to help people change, and to end hurtful patterns. But they also offer a shoulder to cry on and the chance to talk to someone who understands you. And we often don't get this from our partners, whether it's because our relationship has deteriorated or our partners are just too busy.

Think of this as a kind of important unmet need. Sure, "my spouse doesn't understand me" is sometimes just a line, but there are plenty of situations in which it points to a real and pressing need. You may not have chosen the best place to get your need met, but there's wisdom on some level in knowing that you have this need.

Does this apply to you? There's something to be said for the idea that the way you spend your time in a relationship is the point of the relationship. It's even more true that the way you spend your *most rewarding* time in a relationship is the point of the relationship. So to see if this kind of affair applies to you, ask yourself this:

> Do you spend a significant portion of your rewarding time with your lover unburdening yourself, complaining, getting support, being coached, and doing other things that really amount to therapy?

If so, then that sounds like a surrogate-therapy affair.

What does this mean for you? If you're getting therapy from your affair, it might be cheaper and easier to get your therapy from a real therapist. To say nothing of the fact that it might be better therapy.

At the very least, this is a time for you to question if your affair has a more substantial basis than just getting your head shrunk and your mood lifted. But you also need to check into why you're needing this kind of therapy from a lover. Is there something important missing in your marriage or your life?

THE TRADING-UP AFFAIR. A word of warning. I'm about to say some of the least romantic words that have ever been uttered. But I have to tell the truth: We usually marry the best person we can find. Not the best in the world. Just the best in *our* world. The hope that this person will make us happy in the future is one of the most powerful forces in life, and it's called love.

But it's sometimes the case that we *can* do better. It might be that we committed to each other before we revealed our true potential to the world, or even to ourselves. It might be that we had such low self-esteem that we "settled" when in fact we could've done much better. It might be that we were in such a rush to get married or have kids that we grabbed the first person who came along.

None of this matters as long as we're happy. But of course we're not always happy. And that's when we wonder if we could do better. That's also when we find out that sometimes we really *could* do better.

Nobody dumps a loving partner for someone who's a slight improvement. It wouldn't be worth it, given our love, our loyalty, the children (if there are any), the costs and risks of divorce, and other things that tie us to our partners. But if we get involved with somebody who seems to be so much better that the improvement outweighs these costs, then trading up makes sense.

I told you that this was going to be very unromantic. But it is what people do.

Now don't misunderstand me. I believe in marriage. I am not saying that you *should* trade up. In a perfect world everyone would stay in their relationship, work on it, and make it better. But it's not a perfect world. It's the real world. Some people get married for the wrong reasons. And some marriages just fizzle.

And so some people have affairs as a step in the process of trading up. Ms. A thinks she can do better with Mr. Y than she did with Mr. X. So she takes him out for a test drive. *That's* a trading-up affair.

Does this apply to you?

Have you felt for a while now that you can do much better than your partner?
And are you involved in a new relationship because it seems like a significant improvement?

I know this feels like a very disloyal thing to think about, but it can be very real. If so, this is a trading-up affair.

What does this mean for you? This means you have to be very careful. Trading up is a real thing, but remember: When you're trading up you're saying that Y is better than X even when you take into account all the transaction costs and all the risks. People often make huge mistakes in how they go about it. We'll go into this in greater detail in the chapters on how to decide between the two people. But consider two points for now.

One mistake people make is that they vastly underestimate the cost of divorce. Not just the financial cost, although that can be huge, but the stress, anger, fear, depression, and sense of loss that go with it. Plus, men often underestimate how much they'll miss their kids, while women often underestimate what a burden it is being a divorced mom.

The other mistake people make is to underestimate the huge risk involved in committing to the other person. I know he or she seems wonderful now. And may be wonderful. People sometimes say that trading up was the best thing they ever did. But remember: The person you're having an affair with is on their best behavior. Affairs by their very nature are very romantic. But in the world of relationships every new person you get involved with is like a used car without a warranty. There's a very good chance that they've caused someone else headaches and will cause you headaches, too.

So if you're thinking of trading up, to minimize the risk of getting a lemon you'd better make it one hell of a test drive.

THE ACCIDENTAL AFFAIR. No, I understand: If your spouse catches you in bed with someone, you can't say "I have no idea how this happened. I'm as shocked as you are."

But that's not what I mean by an accidental affair. What I mean is that people are often too weak and stupid, even the best of us. It's all too easy to be like Ellie, 42. After eight years Ellie had settled into a solid and comfortable but rather free-from-fireworks relationship with Ned. They were talking about getting married.

Ellie traveled for work—she was a consultant. A year earlier she had been in Manhattan on business. She'd just had a big fight with Ned after a period where things had been a little raw and distant between them. Ellie was glad to be away from him.

That first night Ellie felt lonely in her room, so she went down to the hotel bar and happened to meet a nice guy. It was just one of those things. She was in the wrong place—a hotel bar in a different city—at the wrong time—she was pissed with Ned—at the wrong moment of vulnerability—the day was almost over and Ellie was feeling lovelorn, plus a little drunk.

Some of the other people in the bar were jerks, so it seemed like the most natural thing in the world to invite this guy up to her room, especially since they seemed to be hitting it off so well.

They were an accident looking for a place to happen. They talked, got close, and ended up fooling around. Every step along the way Ellie wanted to say stop, but it seemed so much easier to let it all just happen. It seemed easier to get together the next day than to say no more. And the day she flew back to Providence, it seemed incredibly difficult for Ellie to say good-bye forever, although that's what she wanted to say.

Ellie was weak; the affair was easy. That's an accidental affair.

Does this apply to you? Ask yourself this:

Going into your affair, did you find you were saying things to yourself like "This is ridiculous. It doesn't feel right. I don't know why I'm doing this. I have a perfectly good relationship. This other person's okay, but I have no idea why I'm risking my relationship for this"?

That's a way you can tell that this is an accidental affair.

What does this mean for you? It isn't an accidental affair because it happens accidentally. In a sense, all affairs are accidental—they're not planned.

The hallmark of an accidental affair is that you're not saying to yourself, "This feels so right" or "This is just what I've been missing." If you were, you'd be involved in one of the other kinds of affairs, where you needed something and just didn't know that you needed it.

The accidental affair *doesn't* feel right. And it doesn't feel like it's solving anything. It's a mistake that feels good in the moment, but it's still a mistake, like discovering one month that your account balance isn't $1,379, but $10,001,379. Trust me. You don't suddenly have an extra ten million dollars. Nor, when it comes to an accidental affair, have you found the love of your life. You just have to let it go.

THE REVENGE AFFAIR. Any couples therapist will tell you that one of their most common experiences is being put in the role of judge. "It's not fair," one person will say. "He gets to do X, but I'm never allowed to do it." And the other person will say, "Yeah, but you always do Y, and that's a much bigger deal. That's what's not fair." On some level, every unhappy couple is like two kids at a dinner table fighting over who gets the bigger slice of cake.

Fairness is important for the health of a relationship: There's usually a problem when one person has it much better or much worse than the other. And when that happens you can pretty much predict that forces will eventually come into play to restore the balance.

That's where the revenge affair comes in. It's surprisingly common. When I work with couples in the aftermath of an affair, it's normal for the person who's been cheated on to say at some point, "Well, if he got to sleep with someone, I should be able to do that, too." And sometimes people do just that. That's the revenge affair: the affair you enter into because your partner had one.

But revenge affairs don't take place only as payback. It could be revenge for anything. For being mean or stingy, for example. For forcing you to put up with something you hate, like constantly having to move to a new place. For being neglected. You name it, people can have an affair as revenge for it.

Does this apply to you? It's a mistake to think revenge affairs are entered into in a calculated way. In fact, they're rarely planned or plotted. What's most common is that you've had a grievance. Maybe you're very well aware of it, but maybe you're not:

When the opportunity for having an affair occurs, do you jump in and, as it's taking place, fixate on strong vengeful feelings toward your partner?

It's the sense that you're getting your own back that's the telltale sign of a revenge affair.

What does this mean for you? A good way to look at affairs is to say that the meaning of an affair is the motive behind it. If you're experiencing some satisfaction at your affair bringing you a measure of payback, that's your motive, and that's the meaning of your affair.

Okay. It's not pretty. But at least if you understand what you're doing, you can avoid getting too carried away with how wonderful your lover is. Revenge affairs are mostly about just that, revenge. And you should leave it at that, break up with your lover, and move on.

Then the question is how far you'll take your revenge. Here's my advice. Let this be a kind of cosmic revenge; don't tell your partner about it. It's not only that two wrongs don't make a right. An affair is like punching your relationship in the face. If the first punch didn't take it down, the second punch might very well do so. So unless you want to end your relationship, keep your revenge affair to yourself. Focus, instead, on healing your current relationship, which I'll show you how to do later on.

THE MIDLIFE-CRISIS AFFAIR. All of the different kinds of affairs can happen in midlife. But they can also happen at any age or stage. There's only one distinctive feature of the midlife-crisis affair: It happens *because* you realize that you're aging, you're eventually going to die, and it's now or never.

It's just not true that people have an affair as a kind of necessary accompaniment to a midlife crisis. But when people see themselves age and suddenly feel a kind of panic around the question "Is this all there is?" sometimes the best way they know how to deal with it is to have an affair.

A midlife-crisis affair is rarely deliberate. Many people are living with a kind of ongoing panic about aging; an affair emerges as a possibility, and they leap at it. What makes it more confusing is that sometimes this panic is largely unconscious. Many times people don't realize how much of a panic they were in about aging until they see some crazy thing they've done, like having an affair.

Does this apply to you? The fact that you're in midlife is not necessarily a sign that you're having a midlife-crisis affair. Nor is it a sign if you're in midlife and happen to be going through some sort of crisis—most of the crises that happen in midlife can happen at other times as well.

The distinctive sign of a midlife-crisis affair is this:

Once the possibility has been pointed out to you, can you acknowledge that, yes, you have been very distressed about aging, and that your distress is what's behind your having an affair that you probably wouldn't have had otherwise?

If you answered *yes*, then it's a midlife-crisis affair.

What does this mean for you? Being in a panic about aging is a kind of piñata. It's not so much a thing in itself as a container for a variety of things. You need to figure out what your panic about aging really means. Fear of death? But why would you suddenly be so afraid of death? Fear of your powers being diminished? Well, *are* your powers diminishing? And if so, why? Fear of losing your looks? Fear that you're running out of time to get something you've always wanted, so you'll probably not get it?

These are just some of the possibilities people report. The best thing is to talk to someone about what's going on so you can explore what this is all about for you. Only then can you figure out what you really need.

You probably need something, but it's probably not the affair. Affairs are less a solution to aging than a cause of premature aging!

But you also need to be especially open to the possibility that there are other reasons for this affair. It's quite possible that you're also having a break-out-into-selfhood affair or an unmet-needs affair. They are the most common affairs we think of as midlife-crisis affairs, except for the two I'm about to mention: the sexual-panic affair and the mid*marriage*-crisis affair.

And, in case you were wondering, if you *are* going through a midlife crisis and you haven't had an affair, buy the sports car and skip the affair. It's a lot cheaper. On so many levels.

THE SEXUAL-PANIC AFFAIR. It's a fact of nature. As we get older, our ability to perform sexually can start to decline.

For men, this can take the form of erectile dysfunction (ED). This does not usually mean the utter inability to achieve an erection. Much more commonly, men find that their erections aren't quite as firm, or it takes them longer to get one, or that their ability to get one is more erratic. For some men, even if they have an erection they might have difficulty achieving orgasm.

For women, there are many ways they can experience an increased difficulty in getting aroused. Some just don't feel desire.

Others don't become lubricated as much or as easily. Others find greater difficulty achieving orgasm.

These are the realities some of us face. But then there's how we respond to these realities. Many go into a kind of sexual panic. They feel their powers are declining. They're afraid their sex life is over.

That's when they look to someone new as a kind of sexual savior. They deal with their panic by bringing in a new means of arousal, namely, a whole new person. And this often works. Sheer novelty *can* wake up someone sexually.

Does this apply to you? If you're having your affair when you are aware that your sexual powers are declining, you have to assume that at least in part you're going through a sexual-panic affair. This is particularly true if you find that this affair has reassured you sexually.

What does this mean for you? Okay, you've proved your point. You are still sexually potent.

Now what? It's up to you. You wanted to see if you still had it. You do have it, but be careful about what this means. The newness that got your juices flowing will not be new for very long. And so you'll soon have to face your declining sexual mojo again. Then what are you going to do? Get new sexual partners with ever-increasing frequency? Rent yourself some boy toys? Try to figure out how to live like Hugh Hefner (although even he needs Viagra these days)?

And if you're going to use chemical enhancers anyway, why not stay with your spouse?

The best advice is to not let the sex determine what you do. It's still a choice between two whole people and two whole relationships.

THE MIDMARRIAGE-CRISIS AFFAIR. Like animals or music fads, marriages go through a predictable life cycle. Things are great, or at least good, or at least new in the beginning. But then, after a number of years of marriage, passion has ebbed, sex has gotten boring, and irritations have built up. It's easy to start feeling resentful, restless, and disconnected. And this can happen surprisingly early, around the fifth anniversary, if not earlier.

Another time when the midmarriage crisis may strike is later, when the kids are older, and it's often expressed as "the marriage has run its course." You feel out of steam. Out of ideas. Out of hope. An affair can seem like just the thing. (But it needs to be remembered that there is no marriage course. We're always challenged to renew ourselves in any relationship. We might have run out of ideas, but new ideas are out there. We might have accumulated a lot of problems. But solutions are out there.)

These are the points at which people start wondering, consciously or unconsciously, if they've made a mistake or if they can do better. And so this is when many of the kinds of affairs I've already listed tend to occur. And that's really the point here. This is not a separate kind of affair. This is just a time when other kinds of affairs occur.

Does this apply to you? If your affair has occurred in this midmarriage period (roughly between your fifth and twenty-fifth anniversaries), then it probably does apply to you.

What does this mean for you? *When* your affair occurs doesn't tell you *what* the affair itself means. The kind of affair you're in is one of the other sixteen kinds. Figure out which one it is.

LAYING IT ALL OUT

You probably have a few candidates for the kind of affair you're having. Don't worry about boiling it down to just one. We all have complicated motives, and that means we have more than one reason for having an affair.

Knowing why you're having your affair is a great gift. Knowing points directly to what you need to take away from it, just like knowing why you went to the supermarket points directly to what should be in the shopping bags when you're driving home. So knowing what kind of affair you're having tells you what you need to do about it.

For your convenience, I've organized the affairs by the implications they have for what you should probably do.

When you should probably stay with your primary partner:

heating-up-your-marriage affair
distraction affair
let's-kill-this-relationship-and-see-if-it-comes-back-to-life
   affair
do-I-still-have-it? affair
accidental affair
revenge affair
midlife-crisis affair

And if the kind of affair you've been having points to staying with your primary partner, later on in this book you'll find plenty of help for how to make that work.

When you need to figure out which one to be with:

see-if affair
break-out-into-selfhood affair

unmet-needs affair
I-just-needed-to-indulge-myself affair
having-experiences-I-missed-out-on affair
ejector-seat affair
trading-up affair
surrogate-therapy affair
sexual-panic affair
midmarriage-crisis affair

But how *do* you figure out which one to be with? Coming up you'll find everything you need to determine which person you'll be happiest with in the long run.

It's interesting: There isn't any kind of affair that *all by itself* means you're going to be better off with your lover than your spouse. That *may* turn out to be true, but you can only determine that when we get to the next level.

■ ■ ■

Now that you see how you've been trying to figure out your life and make it better, you're in a position to go to the next level. Figuring out your life and making it better is a challenge, but it's your opportunity to pluck the fruit you've been growing for some time now. It's your opportunity to discover which relationship is best for you.

And that's just what I'm going to help you do next.

THIRD LEVEL

FINDING THE
ONE TRUE LOVE

4

IS YOUR RADAR WORKING?

You were in a relationship with one person. But something wasn't quite right. So you got involved with someone else in addition to the first person.

Now you're involved with two people, and you know that things can't go on this way, as the man said who stood there holding a lit firecracker in his hand. You have to choose which of the two you're going to be with. And you have a third choice. You might choose to be with neither one.

But you know you have to choose.

This has got to be driving you nuts. It feels impossible. Loyalty, hope, fear, guilt, and desire all battle it out in a foggy space where you can't see a foot in front of you.

But it *is* possible to choose, and to choose well, and over the next several chapters I'm going to give you everything you need so that you can feel confident you're making the best choice for you.

The thing is, making that choice isn't easy. At least it hasn't been so far.

TAKING OFF THE BLINDERS

You can have all kinds of people skills and be incredibly savvy, and still there's something about the land of love that assaults the senses and destroys good judgment. You're like a hungry man on a diet walking into a bakery.

Two quick examples.

MANDY AND CANDY. Sam, 46, was a successful entrepreneur. Like a lot of these guys, there was an I-can-walk-on-water quality to him. He came to me complaining about his wife. He wasn't attracted to her anymore. She'd let herself go after the kids came along. She was a nag. She was boring. Blah, blah, blah. Let's call her Mandy.

Then Sam confessed that he'd met a woman he was in love with. Let's call her Candy. Candy was everything Mandy wasn't, according to Sam. Candy was beautiful and sexy. She was sweet and fun. Sam could talk to Candy by the hour. Blah, blah, blah.

But Sam felt deeply conflicted because he had three kids with Mandy, because he felt loyal to her, and because he knew that she would take him to the cleaners if they got a divorce.

To help him sort it all out, first I met with Mandy. I could see glimpses of what Sam was talking about—after all, she wasn't a kid anymore, and she was in a pissy mood, which she had a right to be given the way her husband had been neglecting her. But basically, Mandy seemed okay to me.

Then the day came for me to meet Candy.

Imagine my surprise when Mandy walked into my office. But no! It was *Candy*! Candy, the supposed cutie-pie, was like a clone of Mandy. Candy, Mandy, I couldn't tell the difference. And Candy didn't seem any nicer, sweeter, smarter, or more interesting than

Mandy. It was as if Sam had made this huge deal about trading an orange jelly bean for an orange jelly bean.

Sam had no radar. It took us a long time in our work together, during which he resented me a lot, for him to finally see that he was risking destroying his world for someone who was essentially the same as his wife.

It's stunning how blind we can be sometimes.

"HE WANTS ME." Edie, 39, had no better radar than Sam. She'd been married to a creep who treated her like crap, yelled at her, put her down, and was completely self-absorbed. Then, just when she started feeling her biological clock ticking, she got involved with Jerry. Jerry had one great radar-destroying quality, if Edie'd had any. He was really into Edie. He pursued her, flattered her, wooed her—gave her the whole buildup. That was all she saw: "He wants me."

What she didn't see while she had her affair with Jerry was his anger and selfishness. In this way he was very much like her husband. The first time Jerry yelled at her, Edie was shocked, because it seemed so undeserved. But she blew it off. She didn't see it because she didn't want to see it. And she didn't want to see it because she was high on the fact that Jerry loved her and wanted to have children, which her husband didn't.

But here's the thing. Using the word "blind" might be a mistake. After all, duh, you know if you're blind. But the thing about not having radar is that you think you can see what's going on when you really can't. Sam swore up and down that Candy was completely different from Mandy. Edie was in love with Jerry and didn't tolerate anyone telling her to watch out and slow down.

HOW HUNGRY ARE YOU?

You have to help me help you. I can't improve your radar if you're running around convinced that yours is great. I'll be honest with you. You probably *don't* have such great radar right now.

It's not about you. All the emotions churning through you—especially your hunger for love and your disappointment at not having it—are exactly the kinds of things that destroy radar. I'll use an analogy. You might have very good judgment about what's healthful for you to eat. But if you're hungry enough, suddenly all kinds of crap might start looking good to you. We've all been there. This is when we eat food we regret.

And it's a similar kind of hunger that knocks our radar out when it comes to love. That's what you're hungry for: love. In many ways, this can be the deepest, most corrosive, most mind-bending of all hungers. After all, think of the messes, the *catastrophes,* people create just because they're hungry for love.

But that doesn't have to be you. Remember, my goal is to help you find your way to true love without the messes. And that's where the need for radar comes in.

THE FOG OF WAR

Radar is just another word for "Can you see both of the people you're involved with for who they really are?"

One fundamental radar-wrecking problem grows out of the very nature of the situation you're in. I'll be blunt. There's something about having an affair that makes spouses look worse than they are and makes lovers look better than they are. If you understand this, you'll have taken a big step toward improving your radar.

Here's how it works.

You start sharing a life with someone. However good your relationship, however terrific the other person, everyday life does eat away at it. The stressful responsibilities you live with make you snipe at each other and show you at your worst. More subtly, the sheer "everydayness" of cleaning up the house, picking up the dry cleaning, and getting estimates from painters saps the romance and fun from your relationship. And all this doesn't just happen on top of your relationship problems; it worsens your relationship problems.

Your lover is a relief from all this. The boring details of how and when you're going to get together are romantic. When you do get together, it feels like you've found this bubble of freedom that enhances whatever chemistry the two of you have together.

So here's the radar-fixing question for you:

> Imagine the unimaginable. You're married to your lover with all the daily BS that entails. You're having an affair with your spouse, with all the romance and fun that entails. How do you see the two people *now*?

Does that change how you see things? If so, you're already making progress at improving your radar.

CREATING A MONSTER

Let's look more closely at your primary relationship. Right now, your partner might be a lot worse than she seems, or she might be a lot better. To tune up your radar, let's see which it is.

Clearly something has been missing here; otherwise, you wouldn't have gotten involved with someone else. But here's how the dynamic plays out. We tend to blame the other person for what's missing. This is perfectly normal, but it adds a note of anger and disappointment to the relationship, and it breeds conflict. Your partner is pissed at you, at a minimum, for your being pissed at him.

This is the familiar anger/distance cycle, in which anger creates distance, distance creates anger, and on and on.

So your partner, whom you're so unhappy with, is to some degree *a monster of your own creation*. I don't mean it's your fault necessarily. I'm just saying that your radar is off because the reality you're looking at is off. He might be a sweeter, more affectionate guy if you were sweeter and more affectionate to him.

So here's the question you need to ask yourself to tune up your radar:

> **If my lover just disappeared, and if I put time and energy into my primary relationship, including maybe our working with a good couples therapist, can I imagine a realistic scenario in which things would be better for us and I'd be content to stay in this relationship?**

Most people who answer *yes* to this question feel it is very worthwhile to carefully rethink the whole question of whether they need to end their primary relationship so they can be with their lover.

SEEING WHAT'S REAL. When radar meets relationships, weird things happen. It's just possible that your spouse is actually *worse* than she seems.

This might sound surprising. You're already unhappy enough to go ahead and have an affair. But here's how your radar might go wrong. Let's not lose sight of how guilty you feel. Your guilt can easily lead you to see yourself as a monster. Sure you've been unhappy in your relationship, but, you think, it's because you've done so many bad things that your spouse is so angry and difficult to be with.

Maybe. But maybe he's just an angry, difficult person, and your guilt has blinded you to how unpleasant your spouse really is.

To see more clearly, look back to your days together right after you first settled into your relationship. The period of first love had died down a little, but you hadn't had enough time to screw up too badly. Was your spouse angry and difficult then? If so, then maybe there really is something about your spouse that's driven you away.

And don't neglect the all-important issue of whether your partner has the ability to forgive and forget. If he knows about your affair, or even just suspects it, or if there's even just a good chance that he will find out about it, then your whole future happiness together depends on whether he's basically vengeful or basically merciful.

Just ask yourself whether your partner holds on to grievances for a long time and uses them against you. If so, then based on most people's experience, this is not a good sign that you'll be able to reconcile. A hostile, aggrieved partner is more interested in defending himself than in healing the relationship.

LOOKING UNDER THE HALO

Another huge source of distorted radar is the shining halo your lover comes equipped with. They say anticipation is the best sauce, and that works just as well in love as it does in dining. After all, you long to be with him and, even more, he longs to be with you.

Don't forget the fact that falling in love with someone new when you're already in a relationship with someone else greatly prolongs that "first love" stage.

And that gives a clue about what you need to make sure that your radar is accurate. You need time. Time to see your lover in a less romantic light, under more everyday conditions. Time to knock some of the romanticism out of your relationship.

When people regret leaving their spouse for a lover, one of the reasons they most often cite for their mistake is not giving themselves the opportunity to see their lover as the person he/she really is.

A PLEASANT SURPRISE. You might be surprised to hear that in some cases your lover might be *better* than he seems. Affairs are filled with enormous uncertainty, and not everyone does well with uncertainty. The anxiety of thinking you might be caught, the uncertainty of never knowing when you can be together, the discomfort that comes from your lover's not feeling you're committed— all of these can make a good person much more uncomfortable to be with.

So this is another reason why you need to give yourself some time to see what your lover is really like under more relaxed circumstances. There have got to be times when for whatever reason he'll feel more secure. Well then, what happens?

Do you feel yourselves relaxing into each other and getting closer? If this is the case, then you and your lover might actually be happier together than it seems in the moment. After all, there are plenty of people, both men and women, who open up like flowers in the presence of real commitment.

STAYING HUMBLE

I understand how difficult this is to hear. We navigate through life by trusting our perceptions. I'll go further. We *pride* ourselves on our judgment of other people, particularly the people we think we know best.

But this is incredibly dangerous when you're using these judgments as a basis for moving your entire life in one direction or another. Don't misunderstand me. I'm not saying your judgments are wrong. I'm just saying that they *might* be wrong, and I've spent some time showing you how that could happen.

Figuring out which person you want to spend the rest of your life with depends a lot on your attitude. People who do a good job with this, who end up liking the choices they've made, who end up with few regrets, if any—they may not have better judgment than you, but they have an attitude that says "I'd better not be so proud and confident about how I'm sizing up these people. I'm too caught up in the whole thing. This is a recipe for becoming blind. I need to make sure that I'm seeing both of these people with fresh, unbiased eyes."

TUNING UP YOUR RADAR

What are some more ways to recalibrate your radar and make sure that you're seeing things correctly?

Clarissa, 32, had a thing for tough, scruffy guys. These were usually guys who were born on the wrong side of the tracks. Who knows where this preference came from? Maybe it was a rebellion against her genteel, upper-middle-class parents, but it doesn't matter. This was her pattern. Not that she saw it this way. For Clarissa it was just that some guys are boring and some are challenging.

When she was 27, she married Jake, one of these scruffy guys, and at first she was very happy. But soon the relationship started going to hell. Jake gave Clarissa a tough time about everything. Soon they were always fighting. The feisty attitude that was cute when they were dating became oppressive and annoying to live with. Soon she was feeling incredibly lonely and alienated from Jake.

Then she met Will. Maybe because he was a lawyer, he seemed a little more polished on the outside than Jake, who was a small-time contractor. But this was an illusion. Both men had the same up-from-the-streets background, both men had a chip on their shoulder. Both men were "not boring, because he won't let me get away with anything"—words Clarissa used to describe Will, forgetting that they were the exact words she'd used to describe Jake.

Clarissa was lucky. Her closest friends knew about her affair and did a kind of intervention. They were out together one night after work, and when she started going on about how great Will was, one of her friends jumped in and said, "What the hell are you talking about? Will is just Jake in a suit. If you end up with Will, you'll be making the exact same mistake all over again."

There was a moment of stunned silence, and then her other two friends chimed in. They agreed completely.

Thank God Clarissa was able to let this in, although at first she felt betrayed. She divorced Jake, but she broke up with Will, too, and decided that she needed to work on herself to avoid getting involved with guys who in the end weren't right for her.

THE WRONG TYPE. What do you do if you're attracted to the kind of person who's not right for you and won't make you happy? We can accept this when it comes to food—there are all the foods we like that we know will pack the pounds on or make us sick, so we avoid them even though we like them.

It's much harder when it comes to relationships. And here's why. It takes a lot longer to figure out that the package we like has ingredients that almost necessarily make us miserable. Clarissa just couldn't see that the feisty, scruffy, tough quality that was such fun and so challenging when she was dating someone would mean being with a guy who'd be relentless, mean, punishing, exhausting, and a bully to live with.

When a relationship with the type of person who's not good for us doesn't work out, our instinct is too often to take this as a challenge. We'll figure out a way to make it work! And that's when we fall into the trap of making all kinds of excuses for why the new person we're involved with is really very different from the person we've been involved with. *Will's a lawyer, not a contractor! That's completely different!* Clarissa had thought.

The only thing you can do about this is talk to somebody who's objective about this new person. And your question has to be, "What do you think? Same or different?"

Realize this: The type that hasn't worked out for you in one relationship is rarely going to work for you in another. If you keep being attracted to that type, you need therapy, not another hit of the same old poison. The last thing you need is to turn your life upside down for the sake of jumping from the frying pan into the frying pan.

HELLO, MR. OPPOSITE. Another pitfall is getting involved with someone who seems wonderful just because he or she is so *different* from your spouse. It can be a relief to be with Mr. or Ms. Opposite when you've been having problems with your spouse, but I've seen far too many cases where being the opposite is the only thing in this new person's favor.

I can see you scratching your head. Aren't you supposed to avoid making the same old mistakes?

Of course. But suppose your primary relationship is with an overambitious workaholic who never has time for you. You end up feeling lonely and unloved. Okay. You can see your mistake. But are you really helping yourself by getting involved with an underachieving layabout whom you'll never be able to respect?

And yet faulty radar might lead you to think that this new person is great just because he is so different. Remember: Different isn't necessarily better.

IMAGINE. In all the cases I've talked about so far, the person's radar failed because she didn't ask herself a very simple but incredibly powerful diagnostic question:

What would a life under normal conditions be like with this person?

Yeah, I know—it's a tough question. It asks us to imagine something very hard to see. But I've got good news for you. The people in your situation who save themselves from making a terrible mistake don't have better imaginations than you. They don't have better radar than you. Here's what they have—*they remember to ask themselves this simple question in the first place: "What would a life under normal conditions be like with this person?"*

It's not great answers that will save you. It's trying to *find* the answer that will make all the difference.

FINE-TUNING YOUR RADAR

Here are some questions that can help you fine-tune your radar so you can see what you've been missing. Look, I know they're hard questions, but you don't need perfect answers. It's the attempt to answer that gives you great radar.

Thinking about the two people in your life, what have they promised you, and can they realistically keep those promises?

By promise I don't mean some big, formal declaration. I'm just talking about expectations that have been created.

It doesn't take much to create expectations. Jane, 46, was married to a stingy guy who never helped around the house. She had a long-standing affair with Marty, who seemed to have a lot of money and was enormously sympathetic when she complained to him about how unhelpful her husband was. In effect, Marty was making promises about how generous and helpful he would be. But when Jane finally divorced her husband and moved to be near Marty, imagine her surprise when he turned out to be much more in debt and much less willing to help her than she'd expected.

The two best ways to check out if someone can keep their promises is to look at their track record and their resources. If he says he likes kids, has he done anything to show he likes to spend time with kids? If he says he's a stable guy, does he tend to keep jobs for a long time? If you actually see that someone consistently behaves in a way that's in line with their promises, and does so over a significant period of time, then you can believe their promises. Otherwise, you don't know. Maybe yes. Maybe no. But you just don't know.

And if they have the resources for doing what they've promised, well, that doesn't necessarily prove that they'll keep their promises, but it makes it more likely. Without the resources, it's very unlikely.

Remember, you're much safer and wiser saying "I don't know" than thinking you know and being wrong.

Thinking about your lover, what do you believe this person's exes would say about why their relationship ended?

It's very unromantic but very helpful to think of a relationship as a job, and about someone who wants to be involved with you as a job applicant. Now, if someone wanted to work for you, wouldn't you want to know what their previous bosses thought of them? In this case, the "previous bosses" are their exes.

If you're able to talk to your lover's exes, that's great, but that doesn't happen very often. The best most of us can do is listen carefully to what our lovers say about why their previous relationships ended.

Here are a couple of warning signs.

It was always the other person's fault. Okay, maybe if they've only ever had one or two relationships, it could be the case that they got screwed over both times. But come on. It takes two to tango, and do you really want to be in a relationship with someone who can't see their part in why things didn't work out? And if it really always was the other person's fault, do you really want to be with someone who has no talent for choosing who to be with?

There's a suspicious pattern. If your lover's past relationships seem mostly to end in similar ways, you have to look between the lines to see what was going on. When Gary got involved with Fran, she was a big relief to him because she was so nice, whereas his wife had been so tough. But even though he was falling in love with Fran, there was something missing in their relationship that he just couldn't put his finger on.

Then, one day when they were talking about their previous relationships, Fran mentioned that all the guys she'd been with had somehow mysteriously dumped her. "They just didn't want to be with me anymore, I guess," Fran said sadly.

It *was* sad. And it stimulated Gary's rescue fantasies. But it also made Gary think. Maybe these guys had the same experience with her that he was having. She was nice, but . . . And then it hit him. Fran was boring. Her niceness was an enormous relief after being with his wife, but still. And what do you do when you're involved with someone who's really nice but boring? You don't have a big fight. You just leave. And that's where her pattern had come from. Gary didn't want to leave Fran, but he could see that she would never really make him happy.

They didn't learn anything. What is a great person made of? Life plus growth. A great person allows himself to live, to really have a rich, interesting, and varied life. And then he allows it to teach him something, to change him. Now, it's pretty hard to grow if you don't have life experiences. But there are plenty of people who have life experiences but don't grow.

And that's a danger sign for you. After all, *you* are another life experience for this person. What will your life with him be like if he can't grow, change, learn in response to what he experiences with you?

I'm talking about pretty basic stuff. Let's say that, beyond a certain small amount, you don't like talking about work. You think there are much more interesting things to talk about. So you tell your lover how you hate conversations about work. Can she adapt? Or is she stuck in only one rigid pattern? It's not that you're the boss of what the two of you talk about, but do you want to be with someone who isn't open to doing things in different ways?

SEEING YOUR SPOUSE MORE CLEARLY. You also need to strengthen your radar about your primary relationship. And you have to be careful here. Just because you've been with someone for a long time doesn't mean you see things clearly. In fact, the opposite can be true. We can easily get into one of those weird dynamics where the emotions run so high and the negative patterns get so deeply entrenched that we can't see our partners for who they are at all. It's like when you're really sick for a long time and lose sight of the real you.

To see your marriage more clearly, just ask yourself this:

What are the strengths in your marriage and in your life with your spouse?

If you've been unhappy in your marriage for a while, it can be hard to see these strengths, but do you really believe that they are not there? Maybe the two of you have a wonderful ability to discuss problems and work them through. Maybe things are great when you're on vacation together.

The point is this: It's the negatives in our relationships that are the first to rise up when things haven't been going so great, but it's the positives that tell the tale as to how good and strong your relationship really is. Be very careful about throwing away a relationship with a lot of positives.

■ ■ ■

There now. How does that feel—having your radar all nicely tuned up? I know it was challenging, but now you're in a much better position to begin the process of seeing who's best for you to be with.

5

HOW TO COMPARE AN
APPLE TO AN ORANGE

Kari, 33 at the time, was one of the first people I worked with who found herself in two relationships, with Nick and Bill. But first there'd been Nick.

She'd been involved with Nick for a long time. They'd been lovers. Then things had cooled, but they had stayed friends. Nick moved away, and interestingly, they started getting closer and having more romantic feelings for each other the more they talked on the phone. But officially they were broken up, right?

That's when Kari got involved with Bill.

When Kari first showed up in my office, she quickly laid out for me how there were these two guys she was involved with, how confused she was, and how much pain this whole situation was causing her. Each man knew about the other. Kari knew that both men were barely tolerating having the other guy in the picture, so she knew that the whole thing could blow up in her face at any minute.

At that point in my career I was so confident that I could swoop down and solve her dilemma by just sort of weighing these two guys in the palms of my hands. But it wasn't so easy, and I've since learned that it rarely is.

In Kari's case, Bill was a very different breed of cat from Nick. Bill was edgy, where Nick was comfortable. Bill spent more money, but Nick had more money. Nick was better looking, but Bill was better in bed. Kari liked the lifestyle she had with Bill better, but she liked herself better when she was with Nick. Nick was a better person, but Bill was more romantic.

I soon found myself doing exactly what Kari had been doing. Nick. Bill. Nick. Bill. Aarrgghh! It's like when you look into a kaleidoscope. Every time you turn it, the view changes. It never feels like there's anything solid to see for more than a moment.

And I quickly felt pretty stupid and helpless and confused. This is how most people feel who are in two relationships and trying to sort out which person to be with. The comparison should be easy, you think, but it soon feels exhausting and impossible.

STOPPING GLOBAL COMPARISONS

It took me a long time to figure out why this was so difficult, even for those of us who had a lot of experience and understanding of people. The reason this has been so hard for you is that you've been trying to make a global comparison.

Think about what Kari was going through. She experienced this or that aspect of Nick or Bill, but she kept trying to compare Nick as a whole to Bill as a whole. But you just can't do that. It's a recipe for failure.

Instead, the best way to compare two people is to break the situation down into its different dimensions, and then compare the two people dimension by dimension.

There are, in fact, only four dimensions when it comes to comparing potential partners:

1. Who the people are in themselves.
2. What your relationship is with each one.
3. What your lifestyle would be with each.
4. Who you are with each.

Look at what Kari had been doing.

When Kari said, "Nick is a decent guy, but things are so romantic with me and Bill," she was jumbling together the first dimension ("decent guy"—who Nick was in himself) with the second dimension ("things are so romantic with me and Bill"—what her relationship with Bill was like). No wonder trying to compare two people so often feels like comparing apples to oranges.

You can only make comparisons when you keep the dimensions straight. If Nick is a decent guy, Kari needs to think about what kind of guy Bill is. How do they compare as people in themselves? When you compare people dimension by dimension, everything gets clearer.

What you and I are going to do over the next four chapters is go through each of the four dimensions, so you can see how to compare the two people in your life in each.

With each you might see right away that it just doesn't make sense for you to continue to be with one of the two people you've been involved with. Well, right then and there you've gotten the clarity you were looking for.

In most cases it will become abundantly clear that you'll be much happier with one person than the other.

But there's another option you need to be aware of. There you are struggling to figure out if you should be with one or the other. *But it may turn out that you should be with neither.* There are lots of times when people look back and are very content to realize that the affair they were having was a catalyst to help them end their marriage but didn't really offer them a good alternative. What it offered them was the opportunity to start over with a clean slate.

So let go of your confusion and stress for a moment and come with me. All you need to bring is an open mind.

6

NOT STUPID, CRAZY, CREEPY, MEAN, UGLY, OR SMELLY

Alex, 35, and his wife had gone through a very difficult period during which he'd mostly experienced her anger and coldness. Then he started a new job and soon met Jenny. What a difference. Jenny was warm and sweet, with a bright smile always lighting up her face. Not surprisingly, Alex soon fell for Jenny like a ton of bricks. Faster than either of them could imagine it, they were having an affair, including sex in the office after everyone else had left, in hotel rooms rented for a long lunch hour, on business trips—whenever possible.

But Alex didn't know Jenny any better than a hungry man knows a ham sandwich. Alex only saw Jenny through the lens of what he'd been missing. In a very real way, Jenny didn't exist for Alex outside of his experience of her providing what he'd been missing and much longing for.

"I CAN'T SEE YOU"

Affairs almost always start in a way that prevents you from seeing who the other person is in himself. You're lonely, or horny, or hungry for love, or mad at your partner. Something's not right in your primary relationship. Now here's what happens. You see the new person through the lens of what's missing in your primary relationship.

To avoid this trap, you need to do something most of us never think of doing. Forget how these two people have been with you. Instead, ask yourself what they are like in themselves.

What you want to focus on are the kinds of things that go into making someone a good person. For a long time now I've realized that people who make smart decisions about who to be with tend to choose the highest quality person: the most sane, intelligent, honest, kind, reliable, sensible, generous, warm, good-natured person they can find.

In other words, the person who is best for you is the person about whom you can say that he or she would probably be best for anybody. Someone who is solid and wears well.

A few years ago one of my friends came to me with a tale of woe. She was a great-looking woman with a great personality. I thought she was a catch in anyone's book. But she poured her heart out to me about all of the relationships she'd had that hadn't worked out. It all seemed like a horrible mystery to her. "What's wrong with me?" she asked.

SIX THINGS

As I listened to her talk about the guys she had been involved with, something came through loud and clear. These were all very flawed people. My friend became interested in them because they had some sexy or romantic trait. "Help me," she said. "Tell me what I should look for in a guy."

Fine, I said. Do you have a business card? Write these phrases down on the back of it:

Not stupid.
Not crazy.
Not creepy.
Not mean.
Not ugly.
Not smelly.

You know, a good, solid person.

For the next few years my friend carried this list around with her. And, thank God, she really used it. It's not that every relationship she got into afterward worked out. But she was never again ashamed of the people she was involved with. And by using this simple, clear list, the guy she finally stayed with not only made her happy in the short run but has been able to keep making her happy for quite a while now.

It's pass or fail on every item. If one of the people you're involved with fails on one item, they fail, period. It's not that you're raising the bars all that high. It's that they have to clear all the bars.

So how do the two people you're involved with stack up according to this list?

MAKING GOOD DECISIONS. Let's take the first two items: "Not stupid." "Not crazy." These come together in one concept: The person makes good decisions.

If one of the two people seems to make a lot of bad decisions, about big things or little things, then that's a very bad sign. They're either stupid in a way that ends up causing damage, or they're just weird or neurotic in how they think about things, and as a result make bad choices. They screw up over and over and leave you to clean up their mess. *You can't be with someone like this. They might be fun now, but they will f— you up later.*

YOU DON'T NEED GOOFY. Then there's "not creepy." Creepy is just my shorthand for not being normal around people. Odd. Goofy in a strange way. Off. This is someone who creates tension, who doesn't seem comfortable in their own skin, and who makes others uncomfortable. Who just doesn't mix in an easy, regular way with other people. And you don't need this.

MEAN PEOPLE SUCK. Next there's "not mean." In some ways this can be the hardest to see, because some really mean people have enough polish to hide it really well. One good way to detect it is to look for cutting comments. These might be framed as "the truth" or "being cute" or "I'm just telling you this for your own sake." But in the end, you feel beaten up. And in the worst cases, you're made to believe that it's your own fault that you feel that way.

But you want more than just "not mean." You also want generosity of spirit, having something to give. Someone who has something extra and is willing to share it. When you're with a mean person it feels like pulling teeth to get anything you want from them. In all kinds of subtle ways, they make you aware of their power over you.

NOT UGLY. People sometimes feel that it's very judgmental to be critical of a person's looks. And that's true. Except when it comes to relationships. When you're intimate with someone, looks matter. They just do.

I've known many people over the years who at some point decided that looks don't matter. They got involved with someone thinking they could rise above the way they felt about their looks. But they couldn't. We never can. We shouldn't even try.

The question is, where do you draw the line? And the truth is that some people make a big deal out of things that don't really matter to them. I can't tell you where to draw the line. It's your line. You've already drawn it.

But some of the things that matter to you are really just fetishes. Maybe you've said that you need to be with someone who's blond. Okay. But do you really feel turned off by someone who is not blond? That's where you have to draw the line: where something turns you off.

HOLD YOUR NOSE. As for "not smelly," well, it sounds like a joke unless you run into someone whose smell you just don't like. This has nothing to do with bad hygiene—*that's* a sign of someone being stupid, crazy, or creepy. But there's something about body chemistry—pheromones, hormones, diet, illness, and other factors contribute to this. Research now shows that people give out subtle odors that can be neutral or pleasant to one person and unattractive to another. You can't be with someone if you don't like the way they smell.

IT'S NOT ABOUT WONDERFUL. Notice that I haven't been talking about how wonderful the people are in themselves. That's because wonderful, special, superlative doesn't matter all that much here. Check it out. For example, as long as the person isn't stupid, as long as he has a decent head on his shoulders, that's what matters in terms of whether you can be happy with him. Beyond that, piling on the IQ points ain't gonna make him a better partner for you.

It's the same with looks. "Not ugly" is the thing. Meaning, okay-looking from your point of view. Again, that's all we need to be happy with someone in that department. Research shows that the jump from being pleasing to you to being gorgeous just doesn't make that much of a difference to most people over time.

So how about it? When you think about the two people you're involved with, could you recommend each of them as good, decent, solid, sane, attractive people? Does one seem much better than the other?

"YOU'RE TOO NEEDY"

There's one aspect of being a good person that causes a lot of confusion. Sometimes we reject a spouse or lover because they're "too needy." But is that valid? Is being needy a sign that someone is less than solid?

Sometimes what we label as needy is really a sign of health and strength. I know this may sound like a paradox, but check it out.

Rick, 52, was not happy in his marriage in large part because he felt his wife was too needy. When he got involved with a woman in his office, she sympathized at first. "Oh yes, I hate those needy women." But guess what? Six months into his affair Rick started feeling that this woman was needy, too.

"What's wrong with these women?" he said to me. "Why are so many women so needy?" I was skeptical. You see, I knew that very often when people say "too needy" it's code for "I don't want to have to give you the things you're asking me for." It's like a waiter blaming a diner for being needy because she keeps asking him to fill her water glass.

In fact, being needy can be a sign of health and strength if what it really means is that the other person knows what she needs, and that what she needs is appropriate, and she asks for it. That's not needy. It's called being effective.

And it's not any less effective just because you don't feel like giving your spouse or your lover what they need. People have a right to get their needs met—for affection, for feeling loved, respected, listened to, taken care of. If you're not able to do this for someone, or don't want to, don't blame them for being too needy. Either you don't have much to give or there's something about this person that makes you not want to give much to them.

Of course I'm not saying that there aren't people who are too needy. So where do you draw the line?

One place you draw the line is at "too needy for me." This doesn't necessarily mean that the person is too needy; it just means that there's a mismatch between what you're prepared to deliver and what the other person would like.

Let's say that when you and your partner first got together, she was a teacher. Her hours were predictable and you had plenty of time together. Suddenly she decides to go back to school to become a principal. With her schoolwork added on to her teaching responsibilities, and then later with all the work that's involved in being a principal, you rarely see her. So you complain.

Does that make you too needy? No. You just wanted to have evenings together, and now you don't have that. The problem is that now you're mismatched, not that there's something inappropriate about your needs.

And that brings us to the other place where you draw the line: saying that someone is "too needy for anyone." This, of course, is what we often mean when we call someone too needy. But it's rarely true.

What makes someone inappropriately needy? It's rarer than you might think. People can be so judgmental when calling others needy. In fact, "needy" is often a word used to tell you that you're not the way they think you should be. For example, "I don't like to cuddle before I go to sleep. So if you like to cuddle, that means you're needy."

I think we'd all be better off if we use this rule of thumb: No one is too needy unless the things they ask for mark them as unusual. For example, a woman who likes her guy to call her to check in during the day is not too needy, simply because she's far from unusual. A woman who likes her guy to call *every hour* is unusual. That's too needy.

If you're in doubt, take a poll of ten people in your office. If two thirds of them say that the behavior in question is off the charts, okay, that's too needy. Otherwise, stop being so judgmental and recognize that normal people vary in their needs.

CRAZY CRAZY

We're all a little crazy. But where do you draw the line between normal crazy and *crazy* crazy?

First, let's look at the mood disorders. We all get a little depressed or anxious or too wound up from time to time. Some of us are like this often enough that we can be labeled depressed or anxious or manic. But that doesn't mean you're over the line. Someone is over the line when his mood affects his ability to function and, if you're in a relationship with him, affects *your* ability to function. It's better that you not be involved with someone like that.

I know this isn't a charitable point of view. I know that when you marry someone you marry them in sickness and in health. I know that, and I believe in it. I've lived it. But right now you're in the situation of deciding between two people. Your life is what's at stake. And you owe yourself nothing less than spending it with the solidest person you can find.

Then there are what's called the personality disorders. This isn't where someone has a bad mood. This is where someone is weird and puts everyone else in a bad mood. Here's what to watch out for and stay away from. You can't be involved with people like this.

BUNNY BOILERS. Some of us remember the movie *Fatal Attraction*. Poor Michael Douglas has an affair with Glenn Close, and when he tries to break it off, he finds out that her vengefulness and possessiveness are boundless. At one point Douglas's wife, Anne Archer, goes into the kitchen and sees a large pot boiling over. She lifts the lid and shrieks when she discovers her daughter's pet rabbit cooking away.

Bunny boilers are people who will do anything to get their way. They'll embarrass you, at a minimum. Mess you up. Cause endless trouble. And feel totally justified in doing so.

USERS. It can be so subtle and bizarre when it happens that you can't quite believe it, and so it's easy to just push it out of your mind. I'm talking about the moment that you realize that someone you're involved with is less concerned about you than about what he can get from you.

Now here's where figuring this out gets tricky. Any user worth his salt is going to butter you up, the way the farmer is nice to the cow. Nice enough, at least, to get all the milk he can. So it can be very easy to confuse all that buttering up with someone really caring for you.

But with a real user, at some point you realize that it's really all about what he wants. And what you want is meaningless unless it can get him what he wants. With a user you don't exactly feel like a nothing. You just feel like a nothing outside of his needs. No farmer ever asked his cow if she was having a good day.

MESSES AND FLAKES. We've talked about how wrong it is to condemn someone for making their legitimate needs known. But some people's needs, well, who knows if they're legitimate, but it's clear that they're endless. These people are messes. They may feel like victims, but you can see how they create disasters wherever they go. They make so many mistakes. They take on so much more than they can chew. And they're always playing catch up.

Now, here's where you have to watch out. Messes and flakes can be touchingly sweet. They can be crying out for rescue, and who wouldn't throw a lifeline to a drowning person? But then, with messes, you get sucked in, and the next thing you know *your* life is a mess. Save your pity for the poor people in Africa. You don't want to share your life with someone who is a mess or a flake.

FALLEN ANGELS. They're too good for this world. They're too good for you. They're too good for the second-rate life they've somehow been trapped in.

Now here's how this affects you. Being with a fallen angel means being subjected to a stream of complaints and self-pity that's both annoying and exhausting. But it gets worse than that. Fallen angels will somehow make you feel that if it isn't your fault, it's at least your responsibility to raise them up to the height to which they feel they belong. And if you can't do this, they'll feel it's their job to let you know how much you've disappointed them.

INSULTED INJUREDS. This is a cross between the bunny boiler and the fallen angel. They may not have started out as an angel, but somehow they feel that life has shafted them, and now they've got a chip on their shoulder. They're a walking grievance committee. At the drop of a hat they will tell you tales of their humiliations. You can feel their anger, and their eagerness for payback.

You have to watch out: This type can find you very attractive because you're willing to listen and sympathize with them. And you'll be rewarded for that. They'll be so grateful that they'll do nice things for you that will make you like them. But before you know it, you'll somehow manage to disappoint them. Soon you'll become just another source of humiliation to them. Soon you'll become just another reason for them to complain about their lot in life.

FREE SPIRITS. What's wrong with being spontaneous and free and independent? Nothing. It's great, and enormously seductive. That a free spirit would choose to spend time with you feels like a wild bird suddenly lighting on your shoulder. You feel blessed.

But you're in serious danger. With someone who's simply independent, they're willing to share part of their life with you. It may not be quite as much as you'd like, but it's a real part.

But with a free spirit, they're here today and gone tomorrow. Then, just to make you crazy, they're back again. You never know where you stand. You never really feel that you're important to them. They don't hold themselves accountable to you in the slightest; you don't feel there's any possibility of negotiating their comings and goings. And in the worst cases, you can become obsessed with trying to hold on to them, which you can never do.

POWER PEOPLE. Something I've learned about relationships is that there's one thing everyone thinks about their partner:

"You're much more powerful than I am." We all experience our partners as powerful—their emotions, the ways they assert themselves, the ways it's hard to pin them down. But with normal people all we're really talking about here is being an effective advocate for our own needs.

Power people are different. They may use the same tactics, but the difference lies in the fact that a real power person just wants to win, always, whatever the cost. It's not just that your needs aren't important to them. Even their own needs aren't that important to them, beyond their need to come out on top.

You know that you're with a power person because life with them feels like a constant struggle, you're exhausted from dealing with them, and you don't get your own needs met.

HOW DOES IT ADD UP?

What I've tried to do here is give you some fresh perspectives and hard information. So what do you do with all of it? Without trying to be too analytical, just ask yourself, are both people you're involved with good and solid?

I'd like you to trust your instincts here. If you've started to get a sinking feeling that one or both of the people you're involved with is less than smart, sane, normal, kind, and attractive, then that's huge. It should be the end of your dilemma. If he or she is missing even one of these qualities, you will end up miserable if you get more involved or stay involved. A good, solid relationship begins with choosing a good, solid person.

It doesn't matter how good the good qualities are if the bad ones are bad. If someone is stupid *or* crazy *or* creepy *or* mean it will sooner or later spoil everything else for you. Your decision is made. And what if both people you're involved with fail the test? Then neither one is right for you, even if one is less bad than the other. Less bad doesn't equal good.

. . .

We've just covered the first of the four dimensions: Who the two people are in themselves. Now let's suppose they're both good, solid people. Okay. Next: your relationship with each person.

7

BETTER LIVING THROUGH
BETTER CHEMISTRY

Poor Kenny, 30. His problem was that he had a thing for models. It helped that he lived in Manhattan, where at least they *have* models. It would have been really tough in Butte, Montana.

Not that there's anything wrong with models (or Butte, for that matter). Most of the models I've known have actually been rather sweet. But if you're fishing for love, it's a pretty small pool to be fishing in, even in Manhattan. And life gets even harder for a guy like Kenny when it comes to getting involved with models, because as a freelance journalist, he wasn't particularly rich or glamorous.

Still, if you swing at enough pitches, you're bound to hit a few balls. So Kenny had his share—well, more than his share, actually—of relationships with models. But none of them worked out. There was always something missing, which was confusing to Kenny, because, after all, *these were models.*

Then Kenny met Rebecca. She was trying to make it as a fashion photographer. Interestingly, they first started chatting at a bar after a fashion shoot. They were commiserating with each other about how tough and crazy the fashion world could be. It was a great chat. They agreed to meet for coffee the next day. Then dinner the next night.

Before he knew it, Kenny was feeling things he'd never felt before. He was with a woman he was attracted to, and he was happy and relaxed and engaged. It was very confusing for him. Rebecca was good-looking in a comfy kind of way. And Kenny found her sexy. But she was short and a little zaftig. The opposite of model material. But being with her was wonderful.

Kenny was experiencing chemistry. Real chemistry. Not the kind you think you feel when you see someone from far away and tell yourself that that's the kind of person you want to be with. No, this was the kind of chemistry you have when you're with someone and it feels right. And it's a funny thing about chemistry. When it feels right, it feels *great*. If you can allow yourself to feel it.

And that's the problem with chemistry. Like Kenny, we so often can't or don't allow ourselves to feel it. That's why something that should be so simple—how it feels to be with someone—ends up being so confusing.

If you're involved with two people and you want to see who you have a better relationship with, then you have to see who you have better chemistry with.

THE SCIENCE OF DELIGHT

Chemistry is an important science, because it shows you how to combine two things to make a third thing that's even better. Relationship chemistry is the same kind of thing. It's far more than just having the hots for someone. It's about how sometimes you can combine two people and get something even better.

Relationship chemistry is the science of delight. After all, delight is an important sign of love. We get together with someone because we delight in them and have the pleasure of their delighting in us.

There are only three questions:

1. Is the delight real, or is it based on an illusion?
2. Is the delight healthy, or does it grow out of something that will end up hurting you?
3. Is the delight long lasting, or is it doomed to come to an early end?

The answers to these questions come from seeing the way relationship chemistry really works.

Let's start with the basics.

THE FIVE INGREDIENTS

Over and over, people who are in great relationships report that their chemistry has five essential ingredients.

Now the good news is that people come together all the time, like Kenny and Rebecca, and find that they have these five ingredients going for them.

The bad news is that you need all five. Though you don't need a lot of all five, you do need a passing score for each.

But the good news about the bad news is that if you don't have all five, well, at least you know the chemistry just isn't there. And you're not going to have a good relationship.

The good news about the *good* news is that if you have all five ingredients, you're going to have one hell of a good relationship.

Here you are, now, trying to decide between two people. Don't worry about whether you have better chemistry with one person than with the other. Good chemistry is good chemistry. You just need to know if you have good chemistry with either one. If you have good chemistry with both, well, that makes your decision harder, but don't worry: There are other criteria for deciding that I'll show you later.

Here's how you know if you have good chemistry with someone: You check to see if you have all five ingredients.

EASY CONNECTIONS. To see if you have this, ask yourself: When the two of you are together, do things feel easy between you, and are you able to connect?

There are two parts to this. There's the *easy* part. You know, things are relaxed. It's not a struggle to find things to talk about. You're not worried about making mistakes. You're comfortable with who you are and with who the other person is. It's much more like paddling a canoe in the moonlight than walking on eggshells. It's not that it's perfect; it's just easy.

Of course, if it were just about being easy, it could quickly become boring and empty. That's where the *connecting* part comes in. Along with things being easy, the two of you should really be able to connect.

Let me spell out what connecting means: You talk about things that are really important to you. You're not clueless about what the other is feeling, and not just the good feelings, either. You have empathy for each other. There's room in the relationship for the deeper, darker parts of you.

Too often we have only one or the other in a relationship. Things are easy, but we don't connect. Or we connect, but things aren't easy. When you have this ingredient of chemistry, you have both.

Now let's not get carried away with this. People in happy, healthy relationships have fights in which things are far from easy. Sometimes when we're tired or stressed out or irritable it can be hard to connect. Even the best life isn't all apple pie and ice cream.

So where do you draw the line? How do you determine whether or not you have this ingredient of chemistry? It's almost as easy as peeing on a stick and seeing if it turns blue.

Here are the questions:

When it's just the two of you, and you're able to leave the stress of day-to-day life behind, and you're not mad at each other, does it feel easy, comfortable, relaxing to be together, and do you feel connected, not like polite strangers who happen to get along, but like lovers who are close? And is it like this more often than not?

Now, you have to make allowances for someone who might be feeling very neglected. You also have to factor in the way an affair can make everything outside the marriage seem romantic. But allowing for all that, if easy connections are not present in one of your relationships, and you have no realistic hope of their being present, then your decision has been made for you. *You can't be with someone with whom you don't have this ingredient of chemistry.* Most people regret it if they stay with someone where most of the time things aren't easy and close. And most people who leave are glad they did.

FUN. You might be surprised to learn that fun is one of the five essential ingredients in relationship chemistry. Fun is the glue of intimacy. I know: Sex is important. Confiding deep secrets is important. But being able to have fun together gives relationships the equivalent of whatever that stuff is that holds atoms together and prevents them from flying apart.

I can see you looking a little concerned here. Let's face it, life isn't a ton of fun for most of us these days. Just speaking for myself, most of the time I'm very happy if I can just dial back from *stressed-out* to, well, *not so stressed-out.*

And, of course, fun means very different things to different people. Some people call camping fun; I call it misery. But that's okay. Fun is whatever is fun for you.

And here's why fun matters. It's one of the purest ways we show that we delight in each other.

So how do you tell if you have this ingredient of chemistry, given the fact that life isn't exactly a cavalcade of fun for most of us these days? Ask yourself this:

> When it's just the two of you, no other couples, no kids, no toys (like a boat), and no props (like a party or a club), do you feel that there's always the real possibility that the two of you will find some way to have fun together, and does this, in fact, happen fairly often?

If you're like most people, if fun just isn't there, there's no chemistry, and not much likelihood that you'll be happy together.

It's not about being hysterical with laughter. It might just be a moment when you hear some music that hits you the right way, and you start singing or dancing together. It might be a discussion about politics that for some reason you find enjoyable. It might be just a glance you share when you both notice some goofy-looking guy walk past. I'm just talking about a *taste* of whatever is fun for you.

I don't want you to feel bad if you're not having a ton of fun all the time. Most of us aren't. You just need the realistic hope that fun can spring up between you.

SAFETY. I think you might be shocked if you saw what I see in my work: how unsafe many people feel in their relationships these days. They say: "I just don't feel safe with him/her because . . ." Other words people use instead of "safe" are uncomfortable, intimidated, rejected, disrespected; they say, "I just don't feel trust anymore."

Fear of physical abuse is very important, but it's only a factor in a small percentage of cases. Vastly more common is not feeling safe for a whole variety of more mundane reasons:

- Hearing little comments if you put on a couple of pounds.
- Making the other person mad if you screw up a little.
- Feeling put down if you make a suggestion.
- Facing an ordeal if you talk about something you really want.
- Never knowing what's going on with the other person.

Let's be realistic. No one is going to make you feel safe all the time. Sometimes our needs clash. Sometimes we just step on each other's toes by accident.

But, basically and in general, we need to feel safe in our relationships. We need to feel that we won't be hurt deliberately. We won't be lied to routinely. We won't be belittled.

It also has to do with whatever it is *you* yourself need to feel safe. Maybe it's needing to know that your partner can earn a good living. Maybe it's needing to know that your partner won't snoop through your things. That she won't tell her family about stuff that goes on in your family. That he won't fail to support you if you're being opposed or criticized.

You won't have chemistry if you don't feel safe. But where do you draw the line? After all, people do occasionally hurt and disappoint each other. And the closer you are, the easier it is for this to happen. Answer this:

By and large, do you feel safe being with the other person? And do you feel that you're particularly safe from being hurt, physically or emotionally? And do you feel that you're safe when it's most important to you, when you're being vulnerable or personal or intimate?

Just think about what it means if you can't answer *yes* to these questions about the two people you're involved with. It's bad enough that you don't feel safe. That alone is a deal breaker. But not feeling safe will go on to destroy all the other aspects of your chemistry, and then you've got nothing.

So if you don't feel safe with one of the people you're involved with, then you've just gotten the great gift of clarity. Whatever else this person might have going for him, if you don't feel emotionally safe with him, you can't be with him.

MUTUAL RESPECT. Respect is the least chemistry-like ingredient in relationship chemistry. If you're with someone you find sexy, charming, interesting, fun, challenging, respect can feel irrelevant.

This is where we get ourselves into trouble. Respect does matter when it comes to chemistry. It's essential. Think about it for a moment. Suppose you don't respect someone you're involved with. What does this mean exactly? It means that you don't think they make good decisions. Or you don't think that they understand how the world works. Or that they're lazy. Or that they're irresponsible. Or that they don't have good moral qualities.

All right then, suppose you're involved with someone like this. They might be very cute and charming. Lazy, stupid, irresponsible people can easily be cute and charming. But at some point you start being disgusted. And then one of two things always happens.

You push the person you don't respect off to the margins of your life. You put them in a little box, where they can be cute and charming, but also where all the ways you don't respect them can't do you much harm. This is the way a great many men used to treat women. Many men still treat women this way. Today many women treat men this way as well.

Or you can go in a whole different direction. Instead of pushing the person you don't respect off to the side, you can go on the attack. What you say always starts out designed to be helpful. It proceeds to advice. But it always ends up showering the other person in a blizzard of put-downs. And that's why people we're involved with whom we don't respect so often end up feeling attacked, even end up feeling that they're victims of emotional abuse.

That's how it always plays out. And let me ask you this. Whether the person is marginalized or attacked, how does delight—a fragile plant in any case—stay alive in a situation like this? It doesn't. It can't.

That's why it's a mistake to think you can be with someone you don't respect.

But this is only part of the story. It's not enough to respect the other person. You also have to feel respected *by* the other person. And this is where we sometimes get confused. Suppose for a minute that one of the people you're involved with doesn't really respect you. How would you know? That person's either going to marginalize you or criticize you.

It could take you a long time before you realize that you are being marginalized. How do you know that you're out of the loop if you don't even know there's a loop to be out of?

And if you're being criticized, that can be confusing, too, because it so often comes wrapped in the guise of admiration. Being put down keeps being explained as caring, as being based on a deep admiration for how great you could be, if only . . . If only you weren't who you are right now.

And that's the rub. Be absolutely clear about this. It's not respect if it's only for who you *could* be someday. You can only feel respected if it's for who you are right now, just the way you are, flaws, unrealized potential, and all.

Of course being respected doesn't mean having your ass kissed all day. It doesn't mean never getting feedback. It doesn't mean acknowledging that maybe there's some aspect of life that you're just no good at.

So where do you draw the line?

> Even though you're aware of the other person's flaws, do you basically, overall, respect him as he is right now? Not necessarily that he's a fantastic genius, but that in most ways he's solid, capable, responsible, smart, and kind, and generally makes good decisions. And does he treat you as if he genuinely believes that right now, just as you are, you're solid, capable, responsible, smart, and kind, and generally make good decisions?

So do I hear firm *yeses* to both questions? Fine. But if you can't come up with firm yeses for either of the people you're involved with, then you've just gotten a hit of the clarity you've been looking for. One of the essential ingredients in chemistry just isn't there, which means that you don't have real chemistry that will last with this person. Bottom line: You won't be happy with him.

PHYSICAL CHEMISTRY. It's a myth that people always have affairs because they want better sex. Sometimes that's true, but lots of times it isn't. People often have an affair to get something that's been missing, but who says that that something has to be sex? I've seen lots of cases where a man or a woman divorces someone with whom sex was great and marries someone with whom sex wasn't quite so great but other aspects of the relationship, like the whole emotional aspect, were much better.

But some people make the mistake of minimizing the physical part of relationships. They pride themselves on not getting hung up on something as superficial as how the other person looks or how their body feels.

This is usually a mistake, because the physical aspect of relationships really does matter to us, even if we think it shouldn't. In fact, in my clinical experience, every single case I've seen where someone got into a relationship while ignoring their lack of physical chemistry ended up regretting it.

You might say that you're an exception. Well, you might be. But you're probably not.

So if physical chemistry is important, what *about* it is important?

"Oh, my God, we had the most amazing sex last night." Is that physical chemistry—where you're somehow perfectly matched partners in bed?

Not exactly. Physical chemistry is a little different from that and covers a lot more territory. Physical chemistry is, in fact, made up of a lot of little things. You like the way the other person looks. You like the feel of their skin on your skin. You like the way the other person smells. Kissing feels good and natural. You like to touch each other. You give and receive as much affection—hugs, kisses, and caresses, as well as sex—as you want.

And when you do make love, it doesn't have to be the best sex you've ever had. But you do feel that you somehow have a sexual connection and attraction and interest in each other. That sex between you works, whatever "works" means to both of you.

So where do you draw the line? We can't be utopian—that's just a recipe for loneliness in the long run. But it's not about perfection.

It's just about good enough. The thing is, it's also about not kidding yourself about what's good enough. Ask yourself this:

> Does the other person feel right to *you* physically? Their smell, their touch, the way they look. Not perfect, not necessarily great, but right for you. And do you clearly get the sense that you're right for your partner physically? And does the amount and nature of the physical affection between you feel right? And does the way you make love feel right?

I really don't want to set the bar too high. But you are looking for clarity about which relationship to be in. And if you've been making excuses about one of these relationships and can acknowledge that the physical chemistry just isn't there, then you've found the clarity you're looking for.

YOUR CRYSTAL BALL

There you have it—the five ingredients of relationship chemistry. Here's how it works.

You need all five ingredients. If one is missing, the relationship is probably not going to make it. It can limp along for a while, but over time the missing ingredient will become more and more important, and soon the bad stuff in your relationship will swamp the good stuff.

I know that sounds harsh, but I'm just telling you the truth. You're holding your future in your hands right now. Hopes aren't evidence. The past is over. All you can do is look forward.

The good news is that each ingredient only needs to make it on a pass/fail basis. You don't need an A. I showed you where to draw the line for each ingredient; if you make it over the line, you're in. If you're below the line in even one, you're out.

You wanted clarity, didn't you?

COUNTERFEIT CHEMISTRY

What about false readings of your relationship chemistry? Counterfeit chemistry is all too common.

Here's what to look out for.

BEWARE OF HALO EFFECTS. You know what the halo effect is. Someone has a great reputation, and so for a while all anyone can see are the good things about him. He can do no wrong. His mistakes are overlooked. He'd have to screw up a lot for the halo to slip.

There can be a negative halo effect, too. If someone has a bad reputation, you can very easily expect only bad things from him, and so that's what you focus on. Good things go unnoticed. Bad things leap out at you. It can take a long period of perfect behavior for the negative halo to go away.

These effects can play a role in the way you read your relationship chemistry with both your spouse and the person you're having an affair with.

Sometimes we get into such a negative place in our marriage that it's hard to see anything positive. So let's say you came to the conclusion that you don't have chemistry in your marriage. How can you be sure that reading is valid?

If things were never really good between the two of you, then your reading is probably valid. But if things have been really good between you and your spouse in the past, then you can only say for sure that the chemistry in your marriage is bad if the two of you have had couples therapy with someone you think does good work, and things still aren't better after at least six months.

Think about it. You might feel like crap physically. But you can't say it's all over for you until you've seen a good doctor and followed his prescription. It works the same with your marriage.

The halo effect applies to your relationship with your lover, too. Here the halo effect can make the relationship seem better than it is. So you need to make sure that you see each other under real-life conditions. That's when chemistry shows what it's really made of.

I know that getting to see your lover under real-life conditions can be tough to engineer, especially if you have a family. But I just mean a long enough period of time in which the two of you live the way you normally live, coming home tired and stressed-out from work, having to rush off in the morning, having a day off punctuated by a million chores, having enough time together for the possibility of getting bored or irritated with each other to appear. If you can make this happen, great. You'll learn a lot. If not, then you just need to be humble and realistic about the possibility that what seems like great chemistry may, just maybe, not turn out to be as great as it seems.

A lot of people have ended their primary relationship and married their lover only to find that it was the way they lived—job, stress, bills, chores—that damaged the chemistry in their first relationship, and damaged it just as badly in their next.

BEING YOURSELF. Some people say that when they had an affair they felt they could be themselves for the first time in a long time. But sometimes it's a very different story. Sometimes we get into relationships because we've put on a false front. We seem more charming, more patient, sexier than we really are. And that creates counterfeit chemistry. Your chemistry with someone is only real if you're being yourself with that person. And if that person is being who they really are with you.

All this usually means that you need to make sure you give your relationship with your lover time for *all* the masks to come off before you end your primary relationship.

A VICTIM OF PING-PONG. If there's a problem in your marriage because there's something your spouse just can't or won't do—something that's fun, or sexy, or relaxed, or interesting, or whatever—few things make a lover look more attractive than supplying what's been missing. It's relationship ping-pong, when you go back and forth between two relationships with people who seem like opposites of each other, or at least very different.

But this can screw up your reading of your relationship chemistry with both people. The danger would be that you wouldn't really have two relationships. You'd just have one complete relationship parceled out between two people, each of whom is meeting only a fraction of your needs.

To judge the real chemistry with each, you have to imagine being in a relationship with *only* that person—and with no one else to supply what's missing from that relationship.

THE BOREDOM FACTOR. At some point in any relationship you settle into a groove. You've heard most of each other's stories. You've used up most of your opportunities to surprise each other. If the relationship is going well, we call this being comfortable. If it's not going so well, we call it being bored. A lot of us are a little bored with our marriages.

Then along comes someone new, and being with them is not boring. In fact, it's exciting. But *that's not chemistry.* It's a side effect of how wonderful it feels not to be bored.

You've got to compare apples to apples. The question you need to ask yourself is this: Do I have a very special reason for thinking that *when I settle in with this other person* things will be much less boring than they are with my current spouse?

Some of us are particularly vulnerable to this problem. It's not so much that we're boring people, but we're not good at making life exciting, and the lives we lead don't help matters much. Let's face it: If we're honest with ourselves we'll realize that if life with us isn't going to be boring, a lot of that will have to be up to the other person.

■ ■ ■

Okay, we've looked at who the two people are in themselves and what your relationship is like with each. Those two areas can get kind of deep. The next area isn't deep at all, but it's just as important. It has to do with your lifestyle.

[8]

LOVING THE LIFESTYLE

When people have affairs their time horizon shrinks. You just can't plan, because you don't know who you're going to end up with. The stresses and complications in the present are so all-absorbing that time collapses. You live from one rendezvous to the next, one confrontation to the next.

Here's how Barry, 42, described it. "When I was in college I fell in love with my second cousin, Becky. We wanted to get married, and there's no law against marrying your second cousin. But the family put all this pressure on us not to marry, and we caved. Eventually I married Laura, and it was okay, but she wasn't the love of my life. Because that real love wasn't there, when the kids came along and little difficulties started emerging, we didn't have much of a buffer, and we grew apart pretty fast.

"Then Becky got divorced from the guy she'd married. Suddenly she was free. That changed everything for me. All I wanted was to be with Becky. And that was easy because we all lived in Cos Cob. Becky wouldn't sleep with me until I got a divorce. But we were still in love, and we still wanted to spend every minute we could together.

"It's amazing how much my life changed then. All I could think about was the next thing—being with Becky, getting time away from Laura, preventing Laura from getting suspicious, and still finding time to be with my kids. I was living this almost moment-to-moment existence. Yeah, Becky and I talked a lot about how one day we could be married. But the truth is, the future seemed very unreal."

This tunnel vision that people having affairs fall into makes it very hard to think clearly about what's ultimately best to do. You're controlled by the fears and hopes and stresses of the moment. All you can think of is how it feels to be with this person right now.

You can lose sight of what's most important.

LIFE AS WE ACTUALLY LIVE IT

One of the most important things that gets lost is any sense of what your actual life with either person would be if you made a commitment to one of them and ended things with the other. That's the next dimension you have to look at in thinking about who you're going to be with. Lifestyle.

I've learned something very interesting over the years in my research and clinical experience. I would never have guessed it—I'm probably too romantic. And it's something people having affairs are too *now* focused to see. What I've learned is that in many ways our experience of being in a relationship is our experience of the lifestyle we have in that relationship. That's right. We tend to experience the lifestyle more than the relationship itself, and more than the other person.

Just think about what goes on in your life that has the biggest impact on you. Do you live in a big house with a lot of land or a small apartment in a crowded neighborhood? Do you have a long, tough commute to work every day or a short, easy ride? Do you spend your weekends doing chores or playing golf or going shopping or sitting on your yacht or shooting rats at the dump? Do you watch a lot of reality shows on TV or a lot of detective dramas? Do you have a lot of friends or not so many friends?

It hits you, doesn't it? These lifestyle issues aren't the wallpaper of our lives; they're the very stuff our lives are made of.

A THOUGHT EXPERIMENT

Let me tell you why one woman, Cindi, 37, ultimately, and wisely, divorced her husband. They didn't have a good relationship, but they had a daughter with some developmental problems that required the parents to be unusually involved in her life. If that's all that Cindi'd had to deal with, she told me, she would have stayed married for the sake of her daughter.

But her husband was someone who was tired all the time. This meant that every night at 9:00, or even 8:30, he went to bed. Cindi was a night owl. Even though she got up early every morning to commute to her high-pressure job, she'd stay up until at least 11:00 every night. That meant that every night she'd have two or three hours in which she'd find herself sitting all alone with a glass of wine and a television set, getting depressed and lonely.

That was her lifestyle with her husband. And that's why she couldn't be with him.

So I need to ask you to perform a kind of thought experiment. Suppose you divorced your spouse and married your lover. Then suppose it's two years into this new marriage. *What is your lifestyle like?*

Just think: All those romantic encounters you've been having outside the pressure chamber of being busy with kids and work are now largely a thing of the past. All those chores and responsibilities that used to claim your energy and attention when you were living with your spouse are still claiming your energy and attention with your lover.

So think long and hard before you answer this question:

Do you have a very special and compelling reason for thinking that two years after you married your lover your lifestyle together would be dramatically better than your lifestyle with your current spouse?

Let's say, for example, that you work in corporate sales for a large computer company. You work long hours. You're on the road a lot. Your frequent flyer miles are in the stratosphere. *How different could your lifestyle be?*

Let's say you have three kids whose lives you're very involved with. Plus you've got a circle of friends with whom you get together and talk on the phone all the time. Then there's the church you're active in. And then there's your family—there's always a birthday or a funeral or a wedding or a first communion or a bar mitzvah you're having to go to. If you married your lover, *how different would your lifestyle be?*

Let's go back to Barry. When I asked him these questions it really stopped him. He was another one of these guys who work long hours and go on a lot of business trips. That would never change. And he would probably never have a lot of time for whoever he was married to. So the difficulties that grow out of his schedule would never change.

Barry told me quite clearly that both Becky and his wife, Laura, were really good people. As people, he liked and respected them both.

His relationship with Laura had clearly deteriorated, but it was hard to be sure why. Did they just not have relationship chemistry?

Or was it his lifestyle that made their relationship so difficult? It was very hard to tell.

And although he seemed to have fantastic chemistry with Becky, sometimes fantastic chemistry is based on a fantasy. They'd never tested their relationship under real-life conditions.

So there were a lot of unknowns. *There are always a lot of unknowns.* The people in your situation who get clarity don't do so because they eliminate the unknowns. They get clarity because they focus on what they do know that's really important.

Lifestyle is important. And what was important to Barry when it came to his lifestyle was going sailing on Long Island Sound. He wasn't just some guy who owned a big boat. He was a real sailor. It was something he loved. It was in his blood. If he won the big lottery, he would happily spend the rest of his life sailing around and around the world.

Laura hated sailing, but Becky loved it. She didn't just say that she loved it—all the years before they were together Becky had had her own boat and had gone sailing whenever she could. And doing what he loved with the woman he loved was Barry's great dream.

In the end, it was a lifestyle consideration, their shared love of sailing, that showed Barry that he had to be with Becky. And seven years later, when I followed up with them, they turned out to still be very happy.

But what about your lifestyle with your spouse?

TAKING A LIFESTYLE INVENTORY

You probably think you know all about your lifestyle with your spouse. But do you?

What exactly is it that you know about it? What you know is what the lifestyle is of two people who've grown apart through friction and discouragement. One of you stays home or goes shopping on Saturdays and Sundays while the other plays golf. You're basically staying out of each other's way.

But is that the real state of your lifestyle? Remember back to when you used to talk about playing golf together and staying home and gardening together? That may seem impossible now.

But you can't be sure.

Let me tell you where I'm coming from. Much of the time I'm working with couples. And I can't tell you how often couples have come to me who feel very disconnected from each other. Then we find there's a history of hurts and disappointments. They're disconnected because it's the best way they know to take care of themselves. But if you scrape away the crust that's grown over their relationship, you still find not just the desire but the real hope that they will share a lifestyle together again.

Here's what you need to do so you can get to what's best for everyone. You two knuckleheads, you and your spouse, need to write down a list of "ways I like to spend my time." Each of you should try to come up with five or ten items for your list. (And do this with your lover, too—you never know!)

Whatever appears on both of your lists is a way you share a vision of how you'd like to live. Wherever there's overlap, you have the same lifestyle preferences. If you haven't been sharing those things, it's probably because your relationship has deteriorated, not because you don't have things you like doing together.

But maybe there isn't any overlap. Okay. For some couples it really is the case that there are no activities they can share that they both like.

But even then, it doesn't necessarily mean that you don't want the same lifestyle. Maybe you want a lifestyle where you're free to go off and do separate activities. Maybe the things you share aren't activities but are similar preferences for living in a house with a Scandinavian decor, very clean and uncluttered. Maybe you both like cranking up the air conditioner in the summer, or maybe you both hate air-conditioning.

So don't make the mistake of thinking that a lifestyle is just shared activities. It has to do with every aspect of the way you live. A cluttered house with a lived-in feel or one with a spare, minimalist design? Morning sex or evening sex? A busy social schedule or lots of quiet time? Easygoing with the kids or always on their case? Beach or mountains? Dogs or cats? Chicken or steak? Coke or Pepsi? And sometimes, life with another person really does come down to whether you both like to sleep with the windows open and leave the kitchen messy until the next day.

So don't think about your lifestyle with your spouse as it is now. Suppose, instead, that for some reason the two of you had to stay together and couldn't get involved with anyone else. To be happy at all you'd have to work things out. Then what would your lifestyle together be like?

At least by doing this thought experiment, you'll be better able to compare your spouse and your lover on a level playing field.

PUTTING DIVORCE BACK IN THE PICTURE

There's one more thing for you to think about when you're comparing lifestyle to lifestyle: the impact of divorce.

It's easy to be blasé about going through a divorce. But I'm going to tell you the truth about its impact.

Sometimes—many times, in fact—divorce is worth it. People who study these things have measured marital satisfaction over many decades. If you go back starting almost one hundred years ago, you can see that in the United States marital satisfaction has risen almost every decade. And its rise has mirrored the ease and frequency of divorce. So divorce plays an important function. It gets us out of misery-making marriages, so we have a chance of finding happiness somewhere else.

The truth is, though, that for all its beneficial effects, divorce is rough. It's like a traffic accident. There might be just a bump and a bruise. But sometimes you get badly hurt, and sometimes so hurt that the pain and difficulty keeps going on and on.

If you're going to compare lifestyles, then you have to factor divorce back into the equation. *Is there a good chance that you'll lose touch with your children? Will you lose a lot of money? Will constant hassles with your ex and endless legal expenses drain your nerves and your bank account? Will you become an outcast to your family and friends?*

None of these things has to happen. But sometimes they do. Think carefully about the questions I've just asked. Now imagine that you've gotten divorced, and three years have passed. Can you honestly say that three years after the divorce you'll be happier, and that the divorce itself won't have dragged you down?

Remember: The people who've made the decision you're making and feel best about it are those who refused to delude themselves. And that includes comparing both people, lifestyle to lifestyle.

■ ■ ■

Now we've looked at the two people, at your relationships with them, and at the lifestyle you would have with each. Doesn't that exhaust it? No. There's one more thing to look at. You.

THE FEELINGS INSIDE

One of the reasons Diane, 44, wanted to marry Charlie was that she respected his intelligence and ambition so much. And he had a lot of integrity, too. Overall, Charlie was a very admirable guy. He was pretty decent to live with, usually easygoing (except when he sometimes got impatient). And Diane and Charlie liked similar lifestyles.

Things were so good on all these levels that Diane kept overlooking one way things were very *unsatisfying*. Diane didn't like herself when she was with Charlie. He made her feel stupid. Not deliberately. Not even directly. But there he was, brimming with intelligence, always wanting to talk about interesting, challenging, important things. And whatever Diane said, Charlie pounced on it.

He claimed that this was just his way of "taking you seriously." But he'd question her and debate her, and unless they were in perfect agreement, Diane would end up feeling like an idiot for saying what she'd said.

For a long time she couldn't understand why she'd gone on to have an affair with Scott. Women like her, she was convinced, didn't have affairs, and if they did it meant they were bad people. But whenever she was with Scott, Diane didn't feel like a bad person at all. It was so confusing. Scott wasn't as smart or ambitious or successful as Charlie. And he'd even get a little depressed from time to time.

But Diane felt smart when she was with him. Smart, capable, and knowledgeable. Scott would ask her opinion about all kinds of things, something Charlie never did.

Then one day Scott confessed that he couldn't stand the fact that Diane was still married. He told her that he needed her to divorce Charlie and marry him.

This is when Diane almost took one of those horrible wrong turns that are so easy for us to make. She thought, well, Charlie is a more solid guy than Scott (forgetting that, yes, Charlie was smarter and more successful, but they were both solid guys). She thought her relationship with both men averaged out about the same. (She was focusing on sex, which was good with both men, and on the fact that she rarely fought with either one, forgetting that the reason she rarely fought with Charlie was that she just caved when he started making her feel stupid.)

Diane forgot to put into the equation how these two men made her feel about herself. She'd been blaming herself for the way she felt. And that's where she almost made her terrible mistake, but fortunately, a conversation with her sister, Amy, brought her back from the brink of disaster.

"What the hell are you doing with these two guys?" Amy said.

"Of all people," Diane said, "I thought you wouldn't be judgmental."

"I'm not. I'm just saying that you need to figure out what you want to do, because this is going to blow up in your face."

"What do you think I think about all the time? I just don't know which one I want to be with."

Amy stared at her. "You've got to be kidding. I see you when you've spent time with Charlie, and you're like a limp dishrag. But the times I've seen you after you've been with Scott, you've been glowing. How can you not see that?"

Diane looked away and thought. She'd been focusing so much on these two guys and how she felt about them that she'd forgotten to look at how she felt about herself when she was with them.

And Amy was right. There was a huge difference, and it was all on Scott's side.

Whenever men and women get stuck, unable to decide who to be with, I find it very useful to ask them to forget the other people completely for a moment. Instead, I've found, *choosing between two people is for many of us much more a matter of choosing between two selves: the two different selves you are with these two different people.*

And the fact is that your choice will only work if you like the person you are when you're with the person you've chosen. This is the fourth dimension to look at when it comes to figuring out who's best for you to be with. But how do you do that—choose between the two selves you are with these two people?

CHOOSING YOUR SELF

Sometimes it just has to do with how you feel. That's the way it was with Diane. She felt good with Scott, not so good with Charlie.

But how could she have missed this? And what can we do to avoid missing it?

There are actually lots of reasons why we aren't as aware as we could be about how we really feel when we're with the people we're involved with.

Lots of times it's just habit. Diane was so used to Charlie's manner that out of sheer self-preservation she'd simply stopped paying attention to how she felt when she was with him. She could only bear to be with him when she ignored her own feelings.

And so it is for many of us. We're with someone who bores us, for example. So over time we develop little techniques for amusing ourselves when we're with them and lose sight of how bored we really are, how stale and lame and uncreative they make us feel.

We can do this with any of the problems we have with the people we're involved with. And the result is always that our focus on what we do to cope prevents us from seeing how we really feel.

This is a self-preserving instinct humans have developed. People in prison develop this technique. As do abused children. By focusing on coping, we're often saved from having to see how difficult our environment is.

But the raw data is always there. We know how we feel with the people we're involved with, and to see it we just have to pay attention.

Here's a technique I think you'll find very helpful. Do this the next several times you're with the people you're involved with. Right afterward, ask yourself how you felt while with each on a scale from −10 to +10, where −10 is the worst and +10 is the best you've felt in the past while with someone. Do this several times just to make sure that you get an accurate average reading.

Don't worry about *why* you feel the way you do. That might be important for working on the relationship, but *how* you really feel is what matters when it comes to deciding who to be with.

And here's the rule of thumb: You can't be with someone when your feelings while you're with that person are in zero or negative territory. And if one person makes you feel *significantly* less good than the other, then you can't be with that person.

WHAT'S IMPORTANT TO YOU

This decision has to do with many aspects of who you are. Here are the important aspects to pay attention to. Don't worry about an elaborate scoring system. It only matters when one person gets a very bad or very good score in any of the following areas.

HOW SMART YOU FEEL WHEN YOU'RE WITH EACH OF THEM. You should never be with someone who makes you feel stupid. It's bad enough if the other person thinks you're stupid, but it's even worse if he gets you to agree with him. Then someone who's been polluting your emotional environment actually goes on to hurt you.

This can be confusing when you're involved with someone who happens to be brilliant. But it shouldn't be. It's actually simple. There's a big difference between feeling someone is smarter than you are (but you're still smart) and feeling when you're with that person that you're just stupid.

HOW HAPPY YOU FEEL. This is not about lifestyle now. We've already dealt with that. This is about how you feel inside when you're with each of the people you're involved with. People who are having affairs often think a lot about duty and guilt. You can get to the point where you feel so bad about yourself that you don't really feel that you deserve to be happy.

But you should never feel like this. We *all* deserve to be happy. No form of intelligence is more important than knowing how to make yourself happy.

Stop making excuses for why you're not happy with someone. Barb, 53, is a scientist working in biotech. For a long time she'd been in a committed relationship with Judy, a physician. As the years went by, Barb started missing the experience of falling in love, or having any strong feelings of passion. But she didn't do anything about it. So many women had told Barb that she's clueless about relationships that she'd come to believe it.

Then she met Nadine. There was instant excitement, just what Barb had been missing. For a brief period Barb was very happy. But very soon Nadine started criticizing Barb for almost everything she did, and for almost all the ways she did them. Barb believed that Nadine's criticisms must be justified. After all, wasn't she almost officially clueless about relationships?

But Barb didn't see one simple fact. She wasn't happy with Nadine. She should have been aware of that. And she should have been aware of the fact that whatever her strengths and weaknesses, she deserved to be happy with anyone she was with.

One day a colleague at work asked Barb why she'd been so mopey and distracted recently. This shocked her—that what she was going through would be so obvious to the other clueless types who worked in her lab. And that forced her to think, something she *was* good at.

It hit her that with Judy she was a middle aged woman in a middle-aged relationship, and what was wrong with that? It was what it was. And she was happy there. With Nadine she hadn't really been happy except for the very beginning. Barb realized it was time to let go of unrealistic, romantic fantasies.

So stop confusing yourself. If you're not happy with one of the people you're involved with, stop being with that person. If one makes you a lot happier than the other, that's who you should be with.

Just be fair. It's all too easy to be happy at the start of a relationship. And it's all too easy to fall into a slump when you're not happy. So you need time. But you can't cheat yourself.

HOW HOPEFUL YOU FEEL. Hope is a real thing for us. There are people we can be with who make us feel hopeful, that everything is going to be okay. And there are people who, whether they mean to or not, awaken the feelings of discouragement that lie sleeping in most of us.

Now, you can say that no one can make you feel one way or the other. But in the real world people do cause us to feel all kinds of ways. So if someone makes you feel discouraged, don't blame yourself, unless it turns out that pretty much everyone in your life makes you feel discouraged! Then that really is your problem!

Here's why we fail to notice the ways people discourage us.

In some cases we miss it because they come across as hardheaded realists: "I'm just telling you this for your own good"; "I'm just telling it like it is."

So we blame ourselves. What's wrong with us, we think, that we can't just deal with reality as it's being presented to us? Well, of course we should all be able to deal with reality, but sometimes these self-proclaimed realists are really closet discouragers. What they call realism is a focus on everything negative. They only see the downside, not the upside, and then they have the nerve to put us down for getting discouraged!

The other big way people discourage us is that they're discouraged themselves. They have such a downbeat attitude that it's contagious. They're not hopeful, so it's hard for us to be hopeful. And we can miss this because we blame ourselves for their being so discouraged: "What have I done wrong that you're so down on life?"

It's time that you unconfused yourself. Forget about all the whys and wherefores. If you feel down most of the time you're with someone, then you can't be in that relationship. You have a kind of negative chemistry that will eventually hurt the two of you. It will certainly hurt you.

THE KIND OF PERSON YOU WANT TO BE. Mary Ellen, then 29, came to Boston from Ireland with her husband, Dennis. Dennis was a housepainter with very traditional ideas about how his wife should behave. (This story happened about fifteen years ago. If it were to happen today I'm not sure a guy like

Dennis would have quite such traditional attitudes.) Dennis wanted Mary Ellen to stay home, take care of him and the house, and have babies.

But she had very different ideas. For her America was a land of opportunity in more ways than one. She saw coming here as her chance to break out of old roles.

What Mary Ellen wanted to do was start her own fashion business. She knew it would be hard, but she believed in herself. Then an old boyfriend from Ireland showed up. She hadn't married Timmy because for some reason their families hated each other. Mary Ellen had caved in to their pressure to stay away from Timmy, but she'd never stopped having feelings for him.

And Timmy felt the same way about her. More important, though, was the fact that Timmy felt very differently than Dennis about her having her own dreams and her own life. Timmy gave her all the support that Dennis refused to give.

Of course Mary Ellen had an affair with Timmy, and of course she felt very guilty. So guilty, in fact, that all she wanted to do was slink back to her life with Dennis and let go of her dreams as a form of penance.

Fortunately, a close friend woke Mary Ellen up to the fact that her life with Dennis was killing what was best in her—the person she wanted to be, the person she knew she had a chance of becoming, her best self. And that made her relationship with Dennis impossible. She divorced him. With Timmy she's now flourishing.

As Mary Ellen put it to me, "It wasn't because Timmy was the love of my life. Who knows—when he showed up in Boston it could have been that he'd have turned out to be a jerk. The big thing was that he celebrated what was best in me and Dennis hated it."

So who are you really? Who are you trying to become? We're all in the process of giving birth to a new self that's somehow better than the old one, or at least we like it better. *Does one of the people you're involved with support this? Does one stand in the way?*

Here's the rule of thumb, and I'll make it simple: You can't be with someone who doesn't support you becoming who you want to be. And if neither of the people you're involved with support you this way, you can't be with either one of them.

There's another aspect of being the person you want to be that haunts a number of people. This comes up when someone has already gotten divorced and is now facing a second or even third divorce. People often tell me, "I don't want to be a two-time loser." Part of this is that people feel bad about themselves, thinking that they'd had more than one marriage fail. Another concern, though, is that they'd start dating again, and they would look really bad to their dates because of having been divorced more than once.

But this is a classic mistake of letting a less important priority trump a more important one. A bad marriage is a bad marriage. I understand: It totally sucks that this is your second or third bad marriage. But what can you do? Continue suffering because you don't like the way this makes you look to yourself and others? Absolutely not.

What you do need to do is talk to a professional to see if there's something going on that causes you to keep choosing people who aren't right for you.

As long as you focus on how you feel, and how you feel about yourself when you're with either person, you'll have taken a big step toward getting some of the clarity you were looking for.

[10]

THE FINAL COMPARISON

All right, you've looked at all four dimensions that are important when it comes to figuring out who to be with: who the person is; what your relationship with him is like; what your lifestyle is; and how you feel with each person. Now, how do you add up the results?

If your intuition is talking to you, listen to it. What is intuition, anyway? It's just your feelings, but remember, our feelings are hungry for solid information. Well, you've just dug up a lot of solid information for your intuition to feed on. And you just might have given it everything it needs to render its judgment.

But should you trust your intuition? Yes, with two checks. First, sit with it for a couple of days. Give it time to start feeling even more solid. After all, we've all had the experience of how giving yourself time to reflect sometimes makes an intuition seem like a silly impulse. But if your intuition still feels solid after a couple of days, that's a good sign.

Second, make sure it passes the commonsense test. Yes, it seems right, but is it sensible? You deserve to know.

For many people, this gives them all they need to know about which person to be with.

But what if you're like some people, and you've plumbed the depths of your intuition and come up with nothing?

KNOWING THE SCORE

Here's a scoring system that lots of people find very illuminating. It's simplicity itself. You give each person a score from 1 to 10, 10 being the best, in each of the four dimensions. Then add up their scores. Forty would be a perfect score.

A brief word of clarification. Remember how I said that chemistry is either pass or fail? It is. But for the purpose of this exercise, let's assume that you have relationship chemistry with both people (because if your relationship chemistry with one of the people fails, then you don't need to look further—you can rule that person out). Then, for the purpose of this exercise, give your good chemistry with each a score from 1 (least good possible) to 10 (the best possible).

Here's an illustration.

Suppose you're involved with two people named Chris and Pat. You might give them scores like the following:

	CHRIS	PAT
Who the other person is	8	6
Relationship chemistry	7	8
Lifestyle	9	6
How you feel with each	8	5
TOTAL	32	25

The totals make the answer clear. You feel you have a little more relationship chemistry with Pat, and maybe that's confused you. But when you add up all the scores, you see that 32 is significantly more than 25. It's not a close race. You'll be happier with Chris.

Now do this with your own relationships.

	NAME: _____	NAME: _____
Who the other person is		
Relationship chemistry		
Lifestyle		
How you feel with each		
TOTAL		

Well? How'd it turn out? Was it what you'd thought? Were you surprised?

If doing this tells you what you intuited, that's important information. You'd thought Harry was a better bet than Larry, and now you've had that confirmed. All right, then. That's a solid indicator of who you'll be happiest with. Solid enough to act on.

But maybe you're surprised. If so, don't discount the score. Give it weight. Remember, the score doesn't come from *my* telling you who's best for you. It comes from *you* showing yourself what's true about your life. All I've done is show you how to lay things out. So the score is *your* truth.

But maybe you need more.

Maybe the two people come out with pretty much the same score. Maybe, for whatever reason, you just don't trust the score. Maybe you just don't like making a decision about your life by adding up numbers.

That's okay. At least you're now thinking in a smarter, clearer, better informed way about these two people.

■ ■ ■

So let's suppose the scoring system doesn't work for you. You want a completely different approach. Well, I've got good news. In the next chapter you'll find another way altogether to choose between the two people you're involved with.

[11]

WHAT'S CLOSEST TO YOUR HEART

You've thought and thought and thought, and you still don't know who is best for you. I know—sometimes it can be very confusing. But for some people, one question is all they need to see the path they need to take. What is that one question? Bear with me for a moment.

HOT AND COLD

There are two main ways a relationship can go wrong. There's the "hot" way, in which you have an escalation of frustration, anger, hostility. Voices get raised. Dishes get thrown. And there's the "cold" way. The relationship chills as there's a slow ebb of energy and intimacy, like a bottle of champagne that's left open overnight and loses all its fizz.

Both ways are confusing. In the hot way, the anger-producing problems often coexist with very good things in the relationship.

And then when you make up, you wonder what all the fuss was about. In the cold way, things are never really very good, but they're never really very bad, either.

Carly, 32, was in a marriage that went wrong in the cold way. Her husband, Lew, was a certifiably good guy. There wasn't anything he wouldn't do for Carly, except what he couldn't do, which was actually make her happy. Life with him was just too boring and empty.

Like most people in her situation, Carly did everything she could to make things better, and when nothing worked, she did everything she could to suck it up and make the best of a disappointing relationship. She thought all the time about leaving Lew but couldn't bring herself to act on those thoughts.

"If I just don't think about our relationship, maybe it will somehow magically get better, or maybe I'll somehow magically just stop caring." That was what Carly said to her best friend, Nancy, just before Carly met Jeff. This happening young entrepreneur— he'd just opened his third trendy restaurant—was everything Lew wasn't. He was fun, exciting, challenging, tantalizing—Carly never knew what hit her. I don't think many affairs are launched as the result of long and careful thought. Carly's certainly wasn't.

And then the guilt struck. How could she be doing this to Lew, the best guy in the world? Okay, so he couldn't make her happy. So what? She was clearly an evil, heartless woman, she thought. And yet Carly kept going back to Jeff. And she kept feeling guilty.

"I don't know what to do," Carly said, when she came to see me and proceeded to lay out the whole confusing and (as she saw it) shameful mess.

"What do you want to do?" I asked her when she finished. I feel a little stupid asking this question at the beginning with people who are having an affair, because they rarely know the answer. They wouldn't be coming to see me if they did. But I ask it anyway, because I'm trying to turn the focus in the right direction.

"I want to do what's best. I want to do what's right. It's so hard now. Jeff is starting to put pressure on me to figure out what I'm doing." Carly leaned forward. "This is such a terrible thing I've done. I'm not the kind of person who cheats on her husband."

I believed her. She was too confused and in too much pain for it to be otherwise. "I know. You're a good person who's gotten in way over your head. So try and guess what the best thing for you to do is."

"I can't."

"Yes, you can."

She paused. "Then I should go back to my husband."

"Really? That's what you want?"

Sharply, Carly answered, *"I can't think about what I want."*

A STRANGE PARADOX

Most people who are having affairs are in Carly's situation. They're caught in a strange paradox. They feel guilty, and that tells them that they've acted very selfishly. And, of course, in a way, that's true. When we have an affair a lot of people can get hurt.

But what I see—and most people recognize this—is that they've also acted very impulsively. Thoughtlessly. In a strange way, self-*less*ly, at least in the sense that what they've done wasn't based on a lot of thought about who they really are and what they really need. On the contrary. They've found it very hard to think about their primary relationship. And the affair was usually the product of little thought.

And that's why people so often instinctively resist when I ask, "What do you really want?"

But the fastest, smartest, truest, and most helpful guide usually lies in thinking about this. In fact, there's one question that is most likely to help you get at what's best for you to do right now with this relationship mess you've gotten yourself into, and here it is:

When you think about this whole situation you're in, all the people involved, all the things you think about, *what's closest to your heart?*

This question should tell you everything you need to know. Here's how it works.

We've all seen tornadoes on TV. There's this big swirling funnel of air, and everything that comes into its path gets caught up in it—you can see houses, cars, cows, trees, all flying around inside the tornado. Well, that's what our minds are like when we think about our situation when we're having an affair. There are hopes and fears. Good and bad memories. Things we look forward to and things we dread. It's an exhausting jumble. Then an idiot like me comes along and says, "What do you want?"

Of course you don't know the answer. But you just might know what, in the midst of this swirling confusion, is closest to your heart. Don't think about what you should do yet. Just ask, out of everything in life, what's most important to you in your heart of hearts? What issue, what image, what feeling comes up most often for you when you think about everything that touches the situation you're in?

YOUR ANSWER CAN BE *ANYTHING*

Think before you answer. And please, this is far too important for you to come up with an answer based on what you think you *should* say. It's about what really is, not what should be, closest to your heart.

I've heard all kinds of answers:

- "Jack [the man this woman was having an affair with] is the love of my life, even before I met my husband.

Nothing can change that. He's what's closest to my heart."

- "When you make a vow before God, that should mean something. I really think that what matters most to me is that, by having an affair, I've broken my promise to God."
- "My kids. They're what's closest to my heart. In the end I would do anything for them."
- "I want love. I want someone who will love me for who I am, someone I can love for who they are. Before I die I just want to know that I've found real love."
- "I think my whole life I've been burdened by this huge sense of duty and responsibility. What I want now is to just enjoy life. I think I've earned that. That's what's closest to my heart."
- "It's Kathy. I never meant for this to happen, my falling in love with her. But it did happen, and it's real. My marriage wasn't great, but I thought that that was what life was supposed to be like when you're married. But Kathy showed me how happy you can be with someone, and she's what's closest to my heart."
- "Honestly? It's my dogs. That's it, really."

The point is that your answer can be *anything*. What's closest to your heart is whatever is actually closest to your heart.

FINDING HAPPINESS

All my research and clinical experience show me something really interesting. It's hard to be happy in life sometimes, but in any situation, *if you get the one thing that's most important to you, if you focus on the one thing that's closest to your heart, then* that's *the way you will most likely find the happiness that's available for you.*

Suppose you have a vacation coming up. And it's a big vacation, because for the last couple of years you've had to sacrifice a lot of vacation time. And now, as you're trying to plan your vacation, your mind is aswirl. You want to have fun. But you want to relax. You want to travel. But you don't want to run around. You want to really treat yourself. But you don't want to spend too much money. You want the mountains. But you want the beach. Aaarrrggghhh! It's enough to make you crazy.

Most of us fall for the temptation of trying to balance it all out. A little of this and a little of that. But you well know how often that's blown up in your face, how often a little of this and a little of that don't really add up to you having a great time. They add up to a mishmash.

Happiness comes to the person who can say "You know, there are a lot of things I'd like out of this vacation, but the one thing that's closest to my heart is being able to climb a mountain [or whatever the hell the thing closest to your heart might be]. I think that's what will most fulfill my heart as I reflect back on this vacation." This is a person who's going to have a good vacation.

And if you make the same move in the face of the choice before you, you, too, will have a good outcome.

All it requires is that you identify the one thing that's closest to your heart. Okay, so what *is* the one thing that's closest to your heart?

Some people can answer this question right away. You just *know*. For some of us, though, this question gets the same reaction as if I'd asked you who was the fourteenth president of the United States. There's a swirl of possibilities—could it be Lincoln?—but really, it feels like you have no idea.

But what if you know more than you think? No, I don't mean about the fourteenth president of the United States: You could torture me and I wouldn't be able to come up with that. But this is a question about what matters to you, and you're the world's leading authority on this topic.

And here's how you might be able to discover what's closest to your heart.

As you think about your life right now, and the choice you're facing of who to be with, what are the *five or six* things you can think of that are closest to your heart, that matter to you most, in no particular order?

What kinds of things am I talking about? I don't want to put thoughts in your head, but people have said things like "being with someone who really loves me," "being with someone who really gets me," "having fun," "really knowing the importance of family," "honesty," "being able to pick up at a moment's notice and travel," "being with someone who's not intimidated by my personality," "knowing how to keep the romance alive," "not being bored with someone," "being with a really good, decent person," "being with someone who likes a clean, tidy living environment."

Whatever they are for you, write them down right here, right now:

_____

_____

_____

_____

_____

_____

Okay. Now I'll take you through a process called "forced elimination." The word "decision" is related to the word "scissors." And that's the deal: to decide is to cut away all the stuff that's less important to you, good as it may be, so you can win the prize of discovering what's closest to your heart. And you do this by forcing yourself to eliminate, cut away, the less important considerations.

So now cross off the one item on your list that's least close to your heart. They're all important—I understand—but this one is the least important. Did you do that? Good.

Now cross off the one item on the remaining list that's now least close to your heart. Good—you're down to four.

Then cross off the next item on the remaining list that's least close to your heart. Now you're down to three.

It's hard, but you're zeroing in, aren't you?

Cross off one more. I know it's hard. But just do it.

And now for the hardest step. Can you do it? Cross off one of the last two items on the list. I know. They're both really close to your heart. But force yourself to choose. Go ahead . . .

Were you able to do it?

If you couldn't, don't feel bad. It means it's harder to figure out what's best to do about your relationships, but as long as you're being honest with yourself and realistic about your life, you'll be okay.

But if you were able to narrow your list down to the one thing that's closest to your heart, then you're much, much closer to figuring out what's best for you to do.

The procedure you just followed is very valuable. Most of the time when we're choosing between two things—in this case two people—we just go, Pat . . . Chris . . . Pat . . . Chris . . . What the forced-elimination procedure does is turn your focus inward, away for the moment from Pat and Chris or whomever and on to your priorities, especially your top priority. *That way, when you turn your vision back to Pat and Chris, you know what you're looking for.* And for many of us that makes all the difference.

But why one thing and not many things?

ENDING YOUR PARALYSIS

One guy said to me, "I'm not going to play your stupid game. There isn't just one thing that's closest to my heart." But he was wrong. There was something that really was closest to his heart—his sense of himself as someone full of richness and complexity and subtlety: "Look at me, I'm too deep for your little simplifications."

But here's what happened to him. He got what he was asking for. He wanted to stay true to the complexity of things, and he did. Unfortunately, the complexity of things had no interest in standing still until he figured it all out. Because she got so sick of waiting, his lover dumped him right around the time he was figuring out that she was the love of his life.

But his wife knew about his affair. And when he went to her with a great deal of satisfaction and announced that he was back in the marriage, his wife realized how fed up she'd gotten with all of his games and all the pain he'd inflicted on her, and she dumped him, too.

His staying true to the complexity of things locked him in a time-wasting paralysis that knocked his options out from under him one by one.

And remember, you and I are trying to do two things here. We want to help you see the path that's right for you to take. And we want to help you end the soul-eroding, option-wasting paralysis you've been stuck in. And it turns out that the best way to do that is to think about the one thing in the midst of everything you think about that's closest to your heart.

That's right. You and I both want you to simplify the unsimplifiable.

And, hopefully, you've just done it.

But your work isn't finished. It's one thing to know what's closest to your heart. It's another thing to make the tough choices necessary to get it.

GETTING YOUR DESSERT

Once you know what's closest to your heart, you have to make sure you get it, no matter what. Yes, I understand—this means you'll have to let go of some other things that are important to you. But in the long run they won't matter, because you'll have what's most important to you.

Look, suppose you were coming to the end of a wonderful dinner at a great restaurant, and it came time to choose your dessert. The restaurant was famous for its pumpkin soufflé, but they also had a flourless chocolate cake on the menu, and you love chocolate.

The way to make a choice you'll be happy with is to forget about the choices available to you and just think about what's closest to your heart—dessert-wise—at this very moment.

Maybe you just love chocolate. Maybe you're in the mood for adventure, and you've never had a pumpkin soufflé. Maybe this is a romantic dinner and you're going to want to share your dessert, and you have a feeling that the person you're with hates pumpkin anything.

See? Just by knowing what's closest to your heart right now, your choice is made for you, and it's guaranteed to be the right choice.

How exactly do you go about doing this? Ask yourself which path will most likely give you the one thing that's closest to your heart. And I bet you already know which path that is.

Remember, there are always three paths: staying in your primary relationship; being with the person you've had an affair with; and being with neither one.

Suppose what's closest to your heart is your kids. Well, which path enables you to spend the most time with them and makes their lives easiest? Most people say that it's the path of staying married. Okay, then. Your decision has been made for you. It's always made for you when you go with whatever is closest to your heart and let everything else fall away for the moment.

For most people, at this point there's a big gulp-inducing moment of wondering, "All this agonizing, and now my decision is made by answering this one simple question?" I understand. It can be hard to let go of all the considerations you've gotten so good at juggling. They've been your mental companions for a long time.

But here's the attitude to have. You have to rejoice that you're getting what you care about most, and, yes, you have to mourn the loss of some things that you care about less, just like you mourn the loss of the pumpkin soufflé if you go for the flourless chocolate cake. And it's hard to let go of things we care about. But you'll be okay as long as you remember that you're also choosing to hold on to what you care about most.

By choosing what's closest to your heart, you're choosing the path most likely to make you happy.

WHEN IT'S TOUGH TO CHOOSE YOUR PATH

Sometimes, though, it's not immediately clear which path will bring you to whatever is closest to your heart. What if, like one woman I talked to recently, you say, "I just want to find some peace in this world." Okay. But then you're stumped, because you have no idea whether staying with your spouse or going with your lover will be more likely to bring you peace. How do you sort that out?

If it's hard for you to decide between these two people, you *must* give some thought to the possibility that the best path lies in not being with either one of them.

I know—that's just crazy, you say. And maybe it is. But I've seen too many people who had themselves so convinced that they could only be with one or the other person out of all the people in the world that they worked themselves into a state of desperate, miserable confusion, and then they *finally* realized that the decision was so difficult only because neither option was really right.

There are a lot of reasons why we limit our focus like this, and a lot of good reasons not to.

There's habit: We're just used to thinking about only these two people. But habit is not a reason for doing anything. Good decision makers *always* ask themselves "Is there a third option I'm leaving out?"

There's fear of being alone. At least it's possible to be with one of these two people. If it's neither one, then, you think, you face this awful abyss of loneliness.

Well, look: Loneliness is a real thing, and it's no fun. But here's the truth. There's a lot more to being single than loneliness. There's relief from the stress of relationships that aren't working. There's the freedom to do what you want when you want. There's the ability to strike out in new directions that you couldn't before. There are old friends and new friends. And there's always the possibility, which we mistakenly discount, having been discouraged by our most recent experiences in the dating scene, that we can meet new people, have new relationships, and find someone wonderful and fall in love again.

Finally, we limit ourselves to the two people we have because we're afraid of the search costs involved in finding someone new. In other words, we're afraid of the dating scene. The rejection. The waiting. Having to dump creeps. Agonizing through lousy first dates. And that's the good part!

I'm just kidding. There is definitely a downside to dating. We've all been there. But here's the latest report from the front lines, in case you've been out of action for a while.

With online matching services it's no longer the case that you can't find worthwhile candidates. Even people who I would've thought—how can I put this charitably?—might have a difficult time finding someone to go out with them, invariably told me tales of all the dates they'd been on.

And, most of the time, they're not dates with losers. Remember, you do the selecting. And most people report that even when there's not that great a match you still get to meet someone interesting and have a good time.

And maybe a number of relationships take their first baby steps and then come crashing to the ground. But most people report that this is far less devastating than you think. Or not devastating at all, because you've learned that those false starts are part of the process of finding someone to love who will love you back.

I'm making a big deal about this because if you suspect that you won't find whatever is closest to your heart by being with either of the people you've been involved with, you should have all the hope in the world that it totally makes sense for you to leave them both behind and look for someone else.

THE HARDEST CHOICE

But what if you're convinced that you *can* find what's closest to your heart with one of these two people—you just don't know *which* one?

Jennifer, 29, had had one of those classically difficult childhoods. When she was four her single mother, unable to cope with illness and drug addiction, put her up for adoption. For a while Jennifer pinballed from one foster home to another.

Then she got lucky. A very nice older couple adopted her. They were good parents, and she was happy with them. But she was an only child. And neither of her adoptive parents had family nearby.

So when Jennifer graduated from college she was hungry to have a family of her own. That's why, she thinks, she rushed into marriage with a guy who just wasn't right for her. And she promptly had three children.

It broke Jennifer's heart when she found herself having an affair.

But, of course, this was something she'd chosen to do—things were so boring and empty with her husband. He was rarely around, and when he was around he had nothing to give. And Frank, her lover, whom she met at the hospital where she was working, was a genuinely warm man who had tons to give.

When I asked Jennifer what was closest to her heart, she said immediately, "Family." But here was her dilemma. Was "family" staying with her husband so her kids could grow up in an intact family? Or was it marrying Frank, who had a large family with a lot of sisters, who'd all met Jennifer and been very welcoming?

Jennifer solved her dilemma beautifully, and you can, too, if you do what she did. She understood that when you choose a path, you're not just choosing the beginning of the path. You're choosing the whole path all the way down as far as you can see.

But you have to try and see far. Jennifer did as I suggested. We meditate on all kinds of things these days. So she meditated on what her life would be like *five years from now* with her husband and with Frank. She focused especially on her close-to-the-heart issue of family.

Soon it all came clear. The years with her husband would be an empty sham of family life. Every vacation, anniversary, Thanksgiving would be focused on the kids, and would be bearable only to the extent that she could distract herself from how angry and lonely she felt inside. Yes, the kids would be there, but to a large degree they'd be there as an audience to a charade of a marriage.

With Frank, as far as she could see looking five years ahead, things would be better. Yes, there'd be some weekends and evenings and holidays when her kids wouldn't be with her. But with Frank and his sisters she'd have a large, warm, welcoming family with whom there'd always be get-togethers and barbecues and a ton of cousins for her kids.

Jennifer decided to be with Frank. She made the less common choice for women with kids, but it was the right choice for her.

And that's how you can figure out which path will bring you to what is closest to your heart. All that's required is that you be honest with yourself. No fairy tales, because it's fairy tales that so often turn into nightmares.

You just look down both paths as far as you can into the future, at least three to five years ahead. And you try to come to the most realistic, most likely view of how whatever is closest to your heart will play out. Use your common sense and your life experience.

I know it's hard for some people to do this, but if you can identify what's closest to your heart and pick out the path that gives it to you, then you've discovered an underground passage leading you straight to the happiness you've been longing for.

■ ■ ■

If you're still stuck, I have a good idea why. It might be that you're pretty clear about what you want to do, but you have kids, and it's thinking about your kids and the impact your decision will have on them that confuses you. So let's look at the whole issue of how having kids affects whether to stay with your spouse or go with your lover.

DOING WHAT'S BEST FOR THE CHILDREN

[12]

WHAT ABOUT THE KIDS?

More than a million children every year experience their parents' divorce. But at the giant fork in the road where you're standing, it's your own kids who are your biggest concern, not anyone else's. You're wondering, *obsessing*, about the effects on them of what you're thinking of possibly doing, about how that will affect your relationship with them.

Of course you want to take your kids into account. When people say "I just want what's best for everyone," they're usually thinking primarily of their kids.

But is it true—and is it wise—to assume that divorce is automatically and necessarily bad for your children?

EMMY'S STORY

"Just how bad *is* it with your husband, exactly?"

Emmy sighed and looked away. At 43, she had the sweet but

tired manner of a twenty-something grad student. But whenever she talked about the mess her life had become, her face took on a look of disbelief. It was as if she couldn't imagine anyone, much less herself, being in her situation. "How *bad* is it? If we stay together . . . I was going to say that one of us would probably kill the other, but that's too dramatic. All I know is that it's just awful. I can't stand for him to be near me. And the only reason he wants to be with me is to complain about me and put me down. It's such a relief to me when he goes to bed early, which he usually does, but then I'm up for hours by myself, and it's just so lonely." Emmy started to cry.

"And yet you say you can't leave him because . . ."

". . . because what about Max and Sammy? Their father is a stupid man, and he's depressed all the time, and most of the time he's a bad father. I know what you're going to say. If I stay with Gary, I'm going to ruin my life. And, yeah, I found someone I really love, and I can be with him and be happy and hopefully get full custody of the kids. But what if Gary tries to make me out to be an unfit mother, which I know he will. So I don't see how I can do that. What if Gary gets the kids? But even if it's just plain old joint custody, I don't want them growing up in a broken home. I don't care what you say—divorce isn't good for kids."

And Emmy sat there with a grim, resigned expression on her face. She looked more aged with every word.

MAKING A SACRIFICE

I hear things like this all the time. There's a myth that parents blithely throw their kids to the wolves if a better partner comes along. Of course in this country of three hundred million people there are a few men and women who abandon their children, not just to be with a lover, but also because they have demanding jobs or just feel like taking a powder.

But the overwhelming majority of people, by far, worry enormously about the impact of divorce on their kids, and will suffer a great deal themselves before getting a divorce. The majority is countless men and women like Emmy, grimly willing to sacrifice their happiness for the sake of their kids.

There's no question that being a parent requires sacrifice. There is a question—and it's the question I want to talk about now—about how far this sacrifice has to go and when it stops making sense. In other words, *is it really true that if there are children you should never get a divorce except if there's abuse?*

TRUST AND FEAR

Just by asking this question I'm already in trouble with some people. There's a trend in this country today toward fear-based parenting. Parents see their kids as being flawed and vulnerable. They see life today as dangerous, and so they see kids as lightning rods for disaster. Dr. Spock's "trust yourself" has been replaced by Murphy's Law: "Whatever can go wrong will go wrong." And, using Murphy as a parenting expert, we'd better do everything we can to protect against anything bad happening. That's fear-based parenting.

The myth of selfish parents needs to be replaced by a new understanding. The reality today is that most parents feel willing to sacrifice their happiness if there's the slightest risk of making their children unhappy.

But is fear-based parenting the best way to go? Let's think this through together.

I'm a parent and, recently, a grandparent. I'm also a family therapist. I care a lot about kids. I'd never want to make a suggestion that resulted in children being damaged in any way.

At the same time, here's the trap that a lot of professionals in my position fall into. We want to prove our credentials as someone who cares about kids. And we think we have to do this by publicly worrying about them. If I wring my hands in public more than any other professional, then doesn't that mean that I'm the most responsible professional? And if I'm the professional who sounds most responsible, then I win.

You might say, well, what's wrong with that? The worst that will happen is that you'll be a little overprotective. But at least the kids will be safe.

That's the bicycle-helmet theory of parenting: What difference does a little bicycle helmet make? And if you can prevent brain injury, then it's worth it.

Fine. I'm all for bicycle helmets. But it's not really about the helmets. Let's go back to Emmy. That's some bicycle helmet she's talking about: ruining her life and destroying her chance at happiness so her kids can grow up with parents in a horrible but intact marriage. Is *that* level of protection necessary? Is it even sensible? Is it even protection?

MYTHS AND REALITIES

Emmy believed in something that a lot of people believe in: Divorce always and unnecessarily inflicts significant damage on children. This seems to make sense. It feels intuitively obvious that it hurts a kid to grow up as the child of divorce. After all, the warmth and security of growing up under the same roof with your two parents seems far better than the confusion and stress of growing up torn between two households. And so, this belief says, if you want your kids to be happy, don't get divorced. Period.

But the belief that divorce *has* to hurt kids is a myth.

Let's begin with our own distorted perception. Because we're primed to think that divorce hurts kids, we seize on those examples—and they do exist—of messed-up kids whose parents happen to be divorced and of wonderful kids who come from intact families. But what's really going on here?

It's the old, well-established psychological phenomenon: People tend to notice things that confirm their beliefs and not notice things that don't confirm them. So, for example, if you think Spanish-speaking immigrants are a good thing, you'll notice all their success stories, while stories about the problems they have will pass unnoticed. If you think they're not good, every problem story will register, and the success stories won't.

So what's the truth?

Most books about the impact of divorce on children are based on bad data and fuzzy thinking. The best known of these are Judith Wallerstein's *The Unexpected Legacy of Divorce.* She did a very large study in which she looked at young people who'd grown up in divorced families. What she then did was add up all the problems she could find in these young people. And there were a lot of problems. And some of the young people themselves attributed their problems to their parents' divorce.

Does that sound convincing to you? Well, don't be embarrassed. It sounded convincing to a lot of people, particularly those with a politically conservative "pro-family" agenda. Of course, we all think families are good things, but many of the people who supported Wallerstein believed in a politically right-wing religious agenda. Other supporters were from the overprotective left.

But how convincing are Wallerstein's conclusions actually? She made a fundamental mistake. Okay, she looked at what happened to young people who were still children when their parents got divorced. But in *any* sample of young adults you're going to find a lot of problems. The question is, were the problems of kids from divorced parents worse than what you'd find in a comparable sample of young adults whose parents had not divorced?

Even more telling, were those problems worse than what you'd find in a comparable sample of young adults *whose parents had similarly troubled marriages* but had not divorced?

And the answer is *no*. In fact, it's the opposite. The evidence now is that in families with serious problems, it's less stressful and confusing for kids to grow up with their parents living in separate households rather than with two parents who live like a pair of scorpions in a bottle. What image of marriage does *that* provide?

In fact, there can be something *positive* for kids when their parents divorce. Kids can learn that when you make a mistake, you don't have to stay trapped. So mistakes are not that scary. You can take action when things don't work out, fix your mistake, and move on to a better life.

And that's in fact what happens in the majority of cases. Three years after the divorce, *both* parents are typically happier, less stressed-out, and in a better place in their lives. And that makes them better parents.

And if one of them was a toxic parent to begin with, it's their toxicity, not the divorce, that has a negative effect on the child.

So what should you believe? Let me lay it out.

REAL CHILDREN, REAL DIVORCES

The number-one most important thing to keep in mind is that *kids are resilient*. As long as they get love and support somewhere (probably from you!), they will probably do okay.

Suppose you did research that was the opposite of Wallerstein's. Suppose you found a large sample of adults in their twenties and thirties who were happy and well-adjusted and leading productive lives. Suppose you asked them "Were there problems in your lives growing up?" What do you think you'd find?

I'll tell you. You'd find what Freud called all the "normal miseries of life" in their growing-up years. Divorces, serious illnesses, deaths in the family, accidents, unemployment, and financial problems—these are all the kinds of problems that would have hit them in one way or another during their growing-up years.

In a nutshell, it's not perfect lives that create well-functioning people. On the contrary. The best of us have our characters forged in the pressure, heat, and challenges that come with the "normal miseries of life" that affect almost all of us.

I can go even further. Suppose you managed to create a childhood for your kid in which she was protected from every difficulty and disaster. Never was heard a discouraging word, the skies were not cloudy all day, and not even a hamster died. How well prepared would that child be for the inevitable difficulties of adult life? Where would that child ever learn the single most important lesson we can learn, one that can be summed up in two words: *People cope*?

But you can't learn that lesson unless you go through the kinds of difficulties that make you see that, yes, you fall down, but yes, you get up.

And *that's* why you can't make a fetish of protecting your children from divorce. Guess what? Even Wallerstein agrees with this. In spite of her book, here's what she said to Dr. Charles Foster, one of my colleagues at the Chestnut Hill Institute. He asked her once in public, "Well, but if the parents really aren't getting along, and there's fighting or tension and a lot of unhappiness in the marriage, what should the parents do? Stay together anyway 'for the sake of the children'?"

Wallerstein actually said no, if the parents aren't getting along, then of course they should divorce.

So in the end, the headline-grabbing claim ends in the whimper of a warning not to get divorced for trivial reasons. And that's something I agree with heartily. Especially if you have kids, you don't end your marriage just because doing so will make things a little better.

But who does that, anyway? Almost no one. If you're reading this, it's because you feel that your whole future happiness is at stake.

So what does hurt kids?

MESSED-UP PARENTS

The more credible research shows that it's not divorce that hurts kids but messed-up parents. Most of the time, when you see children hurt by divorce, what you're really seeing is children being hurt by one parent who has a significant psychological problem. It was this parent's issues that made the marriage impossible. But these issues would have had a toxic effect on the kids whether or not there was a divorce.

This can create a real dilemma in some cases. Suppose you're pretty sure that your spouse is hurtful, vindictive, rage-filled, weirdly obsessive, or messed up in any way that might be toxic for your kid. Then what do you do if it looks as though your spouse would be the one to get custody in the course of a normal divorce proceeding?

In this case, the more messed up your spouse, the more you want to get the hell out of that marriage, but at the same time the more it scares the daylights out of you to think of leaving your kid alone in the house with that nut job of an ex.

How do you sort all this out?

You have to be careful here. One huge mistake people make is to think that because their spouse is toxic to them, he or she will necessarily be a toxic parent. Let's face it, you might very well have worked yourself up into a lather against your spouse. So the first thing you need to do is get some independent perspective. I don't necessarily mean experts at this point. I just mean relatives, friends, teachers—people who have had direct experience of your spouse as a parent. If they say something like "Look, she doesn't parent the way you do, but she's fine. There's nothing really wrong with her as a parent," then clearly you're too biased to be a good judge here.

You should accept their judgment. All that's probably going to happen is that your kid will grow up in two different households with two different sets of rules. Is that toxic? Well, the different sets of rules would be there even if you and your spouse lived together. So it doesn't really make much difference.

This is a valuable approach, because the cost of contesting a normal custody arrangement can be considerable. In one typical case, just to illustrate, one woman's divorce was projected to cost fifteen thousand dollars. If she wanted to get a guardian ad litem involved—an expert appointed by the court to examine the parents and the child and make a custody recommendation—that would raise the estimated cost to fifty thousand dollars. But one party or the other is likely to contest the guardian ad litem. That means each side will bring in its own experts. And that raises the estimated cost to well over one hundred thousand dollars.

That's a lot of money and a lot of ill will just because you're pissed at your spouse.

SOME REAL SOUL-SEARCHING. The situation becomes more difficult if the consensus among relatives, friends, and teachers is that your spouse is indeed a toxic parent. In that case, here's what I suggest you do. You need to talk to a good divorce lawyer to get a reading of how the issues you two are bringing up would play out in court. The lawyer might very well say, sorry, I know this is a concern for you, but I doubt that the judge would take this kind of thing into account. What's toxic to laymen doesn't always play out as toxic in a court of law, where the consequences would be denying a parent his or her normal custody or visitation rights.

And that would mean that you need to do some real soul-searching. Here are the questions you need to ask yourself.

Are things really so awful in my marriage that it would be impossible for me to be happy if I stayed in it? What people often forget is the way a marriage deteriorates when you're not committed to it. Then you have a kind of what-the-hell attitude that always makes things worse. But if you knew that you were going to stay in the marriage, then the two of you could do things—including going into couples therapy—that could make things a lot better.

Is my lover really so wonderful? Forbidden love is very romantic, plus you're still in the new-love stage, plus you haven't seen how your lover operates under the stresses of living with you in the cauldron of everyday life. All of these things can make you wildly overrate how much better your lover is than your spouse.

And, most important, does my child have some special vulnerability that would make her more likely to be damaged by the ways I think my spouse is toxic? Here's something you can do to help yourself, maybe save your child from danger, and very likely save a lot of money. Arrange for a one-time consultation with a good child psychologist. Your child's pediatrician or family doctor should be able to recommend someone.

Explain your situation to this person succinctly, and be honest about how you are very likely blinded by your feelings toward your spouse. Make it clear that you really want to hear this professional's honest assessment. And you should say something like "Look, I know you probably would want to talk with everyone involved. But

I'm just looking for your first impression based only on what I've just told you."

After you've done all this, here are the rules of thumb I recommend you follow. But please note: These are just guidelines. I think they're wise recommendations in general, but there's no way for me to know exactly how they apply to your individual situation.

1. If neither your lawyer nor the child psychologist think you have much of a case for labeling your spouse as toxic, then you're best off letting go of the issue. I understand: You really, *really* don't like the way your spouse handles things with your kids. And maybe you're right. Maybe your way is much better. But are you willing to spend one hundred thousand dollars that could help your child in all kinds of ways on a fifty-fifty chance that you can get a judge to agree with you?

And if you are willing, are you very sure that this is based on your concern for your kid and not on your ego?

2. Suppose you get signals from the lawyer and/or the child psychologist that your spouse may really be toxic in a way that a judge can see. In that case, you have to do everything you can to prevent a harmful parent from holding on to your kids. But still, you need to proceed very carefully.

There's an old expression: If you slap the king, then you have to kill him. There are certain fights in which, if you don't win them, you can be hurt very badly. This is one of those fights.

Just think for a moment. Here's a person who you already think is toxic. Then you take action to, essentially, take his or her kids away. If you win, then okay. Hopefully justice has prevailed. But if you lose, you've now made a toxic person feel much, much more hostile and threatened. If you lose, you've made things much worse. Are you still all that confident that you will win? Not *should* you win? *Will* you win?

3. If you just don't have a good enough case, then you need to accept fast and fully the fact that your spouse is going to be your lifetime partner in parenting your kids, whether you get a divorce or stay together. You can't base a coparenting relationship on constant sniping. No one wins, and the biggest loser is your child.

Okay, I get it: Your spouse is a far from ideal parent. But all the arguing in the world won't change a bit of that. All it will do, almost literally, is poison the nest. Instead of there being a toxic parent, there will be two parents who have a toxic effect on their child. And that's a huge step backward.

4. If you're going to get a divorce, then one of the most cost-effective steps you can take that will have the most healthful effect on your child is to have a series of meetings with a good family therapist or child psychologist to work out a postdivorce coparenting relationship between the two of you. I'll go even further. This is not just a helpful step. It should be required.

BETWEEN YOU AND YOUR KIDS

So far we've talked about whether getting a divorce will hurt your kids, and that's very important. But then there's the issue of whether getting a divorce will hurt your *relationship* with your kids. And that's very important, too.

There is one big risk factor. If you end your marriage to be with the person you were having an affair with, and that's how your kids see it, too, and that's how your ex sees it, then that is a public relations nightmare. Think about it. In a worst-case scenario, you're giving your kids the message that they matter so little to you, and you're so self-absorbed, that you're willing to abandon them. At least, that's what it can *seem* like to them.

So how do you deal with this difficult issue? Here are some things to take into account.

YOUR KIDS' AGES PLAY A BIG ROLE HERE. With very young children, say six or younger, leaving your spouse to be with your lover probably won't be something they'll be very much aware of. But as your kids get older, and especially once they're older than ten, this can be something they're very aware of, and very sensitive to.

On the other hand, once your kids get well into adolescence, they might very well be mature enough that you can talk honestly with them about why you did what you did.

THE RELATIONSHIP YOU HAVE NOW WITH YOUR KIDS MAKES A BIG DIFFERENCE. I'll be blunt. It's not about how good your relationship is in itself. It's about whether your relationship with your kids is significantly better than your spouse's relationship with them. To take a classic example, workaholic dads who are frequently absent from the home, and who are frequently irritated or distracted when they are home, are at a big disadvantage. So are moms who are seen as worrywarts and micromanagers.

You've got to be honest with yourself. Do your kids see you as a fun person to be with? Somewhat more important, do your kids see you as the go-to parent when they need support and comfort and understanding? If you can't answer a strong *yes* to both of these questions, then there's an added risk that your relationship with your kids might deteriorate.

HAS IT BEEN CLEAR TO YOUR KIDS THAT THERE'S A SERIOUS PROBLEM IN YOUR MARRIAGE ABOVE AND BEYOND THIS OTHER RELATIONSHIP OF YOURS? This is where you can prevent things from deteriorating in many cases, but you have to play it very carefully. Let's look at what's true. Your affair didn't make your marriage bad. On the contrary. You were vulnerable to getting involved with someone because there were real problems in your marriage. Well, then, your kids need to know about these marital problems.

But use caution. You can't make it sound as if you're trashing your spouse. So your description of "the problems" has to be filled with the word "we": "We just couldn't get along"; "We just wanted such different things from life"; "We didn't know how to make each other happy"; "We were never a good fit for each other"; "We fought all the time."

And you can't be too explicit, either, particularly when you're talking about sexual problems. But you do need to be explicit enough on your side so that you make a more compelling case than "that selfish bastard of a father of yours got involved with this slut and destroyed our family," which might be your spouse's case.

Clearly, if you can't make an overwhelming case for why it was your bad marriage rather than your affair that led to your divorce, then there's a real risk of your relationship with your kids deteriorating.

HOW VINDICTIVE IS YOUR SPOUSE? You can never tell about people. Some very sweet-seeming people can be so hurt that they turn vindictive. Some real tough characters can decide that what's in their kids' best interest must rule and so they will never utter a vindictive word. Here are the four factors to look at:

1. How betrayed does your spouse feel?
2. How able is your spouse to understand and take responsibility for a 50 percent share in creating the marriage problems?
3. Does your spouse have a vengeful, punishing nature?
4. Does your spouse easily sacrifice her emotional needs in the moment for the sake of what's best for your kids?

Looking at these four factors, does it look to you as though you're quite possibly facing the reality of a vindictive spouse? Putting that together with your answers to the other questions, you should now have a much clearer sense of how likely it is that your relationship with your kids will deteriorate if you get a divorce, given the fact that you've had an affair.

But what do you *do* about it? It's not obvious.

JUST DON'T DECEIVE YOURSELF

Compare these two scenarios.

Joe, 51, realizes he could have been there more for his two sons, 15 and 17. He thinks that may be a large part of the reason they got so incredibly angry with him when they learned he was having an affair. But his marriage had been an absolute disaster. Since before the first child was born he knew he would never be happy in this marriage—they had a child, and then another child, in a desperate attempt to make things better, but of course this "solution" always fails.

It's been very painful to think about leaving and having his sons be furious with him, but he's hung in there for years, and he knows they appreciate the way he's given them most of what he had to give, and he recognizes that they'll be out of the house in a very short time anyway. Plus, he's been with his lover for a long time, and he's absolutely confident that she can make him happy. So Joe is willing to take the risk of a short-term deterioration in his relationship with his sons. He has good reason to believe that he and his sons will remain close.

Things are very different for Marge, 37. Her daughter, Chloe, 7, has been diagnosed with a mild case of Asperger's syndrome. She's totally mainstreamed in school, but she clearly has some special needs. She has a difficult time with any kind of separation.

In addition, Marge feels that her husband is the kind of guy who's so protective of Chloe that he might very well become retaliatory if Marge leaves the marriage because of this guy she's been involved with. But while their marriage has been a disappointment, it's not horrible. Nor is the guy she's having an affair with turning out to be so wonderful. So Marge doesn't feel she can jeopardize her relationship with her daughter. Chloe needs her too much, and the marriage just isn't that bad.

So, in the end, when kids are involved, it's a judgment call on your part. The key thing is not to deceive yourself. If there's a potential for your relationship with your kids to deteriorate, then you have to face that and weigh it in the balance. And if your marriage is really bad, and your lover is really terrific, then you have to face that and be willing to ask yourself if a lifetime of misery if you stay married is worth it for the sake of a measurable but not large and probably not permanent deterioration in your relationship with your kids.

WHAT THE BEST PARENTS DO

You have a responsibility as a parent to be there for your kids, and to avoid hurting them. That's obvious. But, equally, you have a responsibility to yourself to lead a life that's worth living. You can't neglect either responsibility.

The people who decided to get divorced when they have kids, and are happy about the choice they made, all have one thing in common. They are the people who were absolutely honest with themselves and absolutely clear-sighted about the realities they were dealing with. The people who weren't happy with their decision were the ones who kept their heads in the sand and failed to read the signs that were clearly there.

That's what made all the difference. It's incredibly difficult, so of course you're going to agonize over it. But honesty and clear-sightedness will help you do what's best for everyone. And the material in this chapter will show you what you need to keep in mind.

If you're wondering how to deal with the kids as you go through the divorce process, there's a section at the end of this book that gives you a quick course in how best to handle everything that will come up.

. . .

By this point, most people have a clear sense of who's best for them. But suppose that, in spite of all you've learned, you still aren't sure.

I'll tell you what's probably going on, based on my experience. I think you do know. I think you see it very clearly. But I think you find the process of acting on your choice very daunting.

I see this a lot, not just when it comes to deciding whether to be with your spouse or your lover, but in many other life-shifting decisions.

Suppose you have a funny-looking mole somewhere on your body that's starting to give you some concern. Of course if you're a hypochondriac you run to the doctor immediately. But a lot of us respond very differently.

Though we know that the responsible thing to do is to get it checked out, the thought of having expensive tests, and then maybe having to deal with a diagnosis of cancer, and then having to deal with the ordeal of being treated, and the fear of death—yikes! Well, we still know what we should do, but we put it off.

Because we find doing what we should do so daunting, the medical establishment works at making it less so: "Look, it's probably nothing, but even if it is something, the sooner you deal with it, the more likely you are to treat it successfully."

So whenever you're not acting on a choice that you know is best, the key is to look at what makes it daunting and to make it less daunting. That's what we're going to do next. We're going to look at how to act on your choice—whatever it is—so we can take the fear out of it.

So come along with me, and even if you still don't think you know what's best, I'm betting that by the time you see how to make your choice in the best possible way, you'll also be able to say who's right for you.

FIFTH LEVEL

BREAKING UP
THE TRIANGLE

[13]

MAKING A CLEAN BREAK

If there's one message I've been trying to drive home, it's that the truth will set you free. As long as you're having an affair, you're caught in limbo between two relationships. I understand: In some ways, that's good. Affairs often balance things out by meeting some need that's not being met in your primary relationship. But as the months go by it almost always gets clearer and clearer that you're in an untenable no-man's-land, caught between two partial relationships.

But there is a truth about who it's best for you to be with. It's not a truth about how everything will be wonderful and perfect with one person. You probably weren't born with a billion-dollar trust fund, either. But it is a truth that points to how you can be far happier than you are now.

A big reason people sometimes can't see the truth that will set them free is the fact that it points to a breakup with one of the people they're involved with, and they just can't face that.

In fact, it can be pretty scary.

When San Francisco first started allowing civil unions for gay couples, James, 37, very much wanted to get hitched to his long-time partner, Brad. But just as with so many straight couples, there was more to their relationship than met the eye. James and Brad had had a rocky relationship. Eleven years younger than Brad, James had looked up to him as a mentor as well as a lover and partner. But they'd clearly grown apart. James suspected that for Brad the best thing about their relationship had been the idea of bringing along a young man, and now that James was no longer so young, Brad was losing interest. But Brad was that much older himself, and James felt that that was why Brad was afraid of making a break.

James hoped that their civil union, being a kind of marriage, would cement their relationship. It didn't. Soon Brad started acting cold again. And although he had told himself that he would never do this, James had an affair with a fellow employee at the insurance company where he worked, which soon turned into an emotional relationship as well.

"I wish he would hit me," James told me, talking about Brad. "It would make breaking up so much easier."

And that's the place a lot of us are in, even if we wouldn't put it in quite those words. James saw the truth. It was over with Brad, and he wanted to be with his new guy. But to break up with someone he loved, with whom he'd shared most of his adult life—that was hard. Too hard. Too hard for James to set himself free.

But *was* it too hard? Yes, the pain and stress of a breakup are always difficult, but James had gotten stuck where most of us get stuck. He wondered, *What do I say? How do I say it? When do I say it? How do I set things up so things go as smoothly as possible?*

It turns out that there are good answers to all these questions.

CUTTING THE CORD

Breaking up with someone is like giving birth to a baby. It's actually not all that complicated. In some parts of the world, women do it all by themselves—giving birth, that is. It's just that there are certain ways things can go wrong, and they're what cause all the problems. So let's see what we can do to prevent these things from going wrong. Okay?

When you tell someone that you want to break up with them, their first response is almost always "Why?" That question contains a terrible trap. Trying to answer it is the first mistake to avoid. *Don't answer the question why, and especially don't go into details.*

I want you to hear this loud and clear. A breakup is *not* a discussion about how you can patch up your relationship. As I said at the beginning of this book, you should have already made a serious effort to make your relationship as good as it can be. You should have already proved that trying to patch things up isn't going to work.

Most of the misery in breakups come because people unwittingly turn the breakup into an attempted "patchup." And they do this by getting sucked into answering the question "Why?"

Almost any possible answer to the question why can easily slide into a discussion about how to patch things up.

- "Because we fight all the time." *Response:* "We'll find a really good couples therapist this time and really, really work on our relationship."
- "Because we've drifted apart." *Response:* "We just need to spend time together and work on developing interests we have in common."
- "Because you slept with my sister." *Response:* "I'll make it up to you, and I'll never do that again."

- "Because we just don't get along." *Response:* "But things aren't as bad as you think. . . ."
- "Because you're ugly." *Response:* "I'll lose weight and get a face-lift."

And on it goes. But it doesn't stop there. Oh no. You find yourself explaining why a face-lift or making it up to you won't be enough or won't work. And then, of course, the other person offers to go even further. Or else he turns the tables and starts talking about how it's really all your fault.

One way or another, you get sucked into a negotiation about your relationship. Before you know it you realize that you're faced with two alternatives. You can say "I don't want to be with you under any circumstances." That ends the painful pulling back and forth. But in the meantime the discussing and negotiating have heartbreakingly gone on for hours, days, months, sometimes years. What a waste.

The other alternative is that you cave. At some point you seize on some little suggestion: "Yes! You're right! We'll get a dog! That will be so much fun, and we'll go for walks and everything, and we'll get close again."

But why did you cave? Because you were worn-out.

So here's the rule of thumb. You should have already made an all-out effort to make things the best they can be. But if the help doesn't help or if the best just isn't good enough, then the days of patching things up are over. And then you need to break up. But you don't need to give an explanation, and you shouldn't give one, because it will just lead you into an attempt to patch things up.

So what do you say to break up with someone? All you say is "This relationship just doesn't work for me anymore." And if they ask "Why not?" the answer is "Because it just doesn't work for me." Repeat these words as often as necessary. Don't add any details to this clear statement.

Keep trying to change the subject to when and how you're going to separate.

I know this might sound harsh and cruel and cold. But look, there may very well be a time for the two of you to hold each other and cry and mourn the loss of your relationship. That would be a good thing to do later. But breaking up the way I'm suggesting is far less harsh than an endlessly dragged out and much more painful discussion that involves a lot of desperate begging that can never really lead anywhere good. And it's far better than a time-wasting, heart-eroding period where you cave into the idea of working on a relationship you don't want to stay in.

So the rule of thumb is this. Don't say it's over until you're *sure* it's over. That's why you don't want to be one of those people who are always threatening to end things. But if you are sure it's over, then all you need to say is "It's over."

NO WEASELS

In case you're thinking "You're just nuts if you think that all I'm going to do is say 'It just doesn't work for me' and that's going to be the end of the discussion," you're right. I would be nuts if I thought that. You want to cause as little pain as possible, and yet there is a lot to talk about. So how do you go about it?

The principle is pretty simple: *Tell the truth, but meet their need.*

Let me unpack this a little. Most of us think we have a choice only between a cruel truth ("There's no good way to put this, so I'll just come right out and say it . . .") and a weasely lie ("I'm just going out for a loaf of bread," even though you have no intention of ever coming back).

But there is an optimal choice. It's where you tell the truth, but you think as carefully and deeply as you can about what the other person hearing your truth would need when she hears it. And then, as part of the process of telling your truth, you find a way to address their need.

Quick example. "Do I look fat in these pants?"

"Well, they're not the most flattering pants I've ever seen on you, but I love you, and I think you're beautiful."

Another example. If I asked you to spend a weekend at my house helping me move, you could respond with a cruel truth ("I'm just not interested, cupcake") or with a weasely lie ("Sure," and then not show up). Or you could tell the truth and meet my need for help with my move: "It's just not a good weekend for me, but why not ask Joey? He's free, and he might be happy to help if you buy him dinner."

Breaking up with someone is a much bigger deal, but the principle is the same. What needs do you think your spouse or lover will have if you tell them that you're ending your relationship with them? You have no right telling them that until you make an honest attempt to figure out their needs and try to hit on a way to address them.

To help you, here are the most common needs people have when someone breaks up with them:

- To know what your future relationship will be.
- To know that you can still be friends.
- To know how the money is going to work.
- To know where he/she is going to live.
- To know how much time he/she has before you separate.
- To know who's going to have custody of the kids.
- To know who's going to have custody of the dog.
- To know what you're going to tell the kids.
- To know how you're going to explain this to family and friends.
- To know what the next steps are and what the timeline is.
- To know that there's nothing they could've done to change things.

These are all real and valid needs. The only need you refuse to meet is their need to know why.

Now here's the really interesting part. You can't know for sure what the other person is going to need when you say that you want to break up. But you're trying to minimize pain, not be perfect. And I've found over the years that you minimize pain by honestly doing your best to guess what the other's needs are. You might not guess exactly right, but that's okay. And by trying, you're doing the most you can to show that you have goodwill.

NO SCENES

The question everyone asks is, "Is there a way to break up with someone without there having to be a scene?" That's the Holy Grail: the pain-free, scene-free breakup. And we look for it because we hate confrontations, which is just a polite way of saying that most of us are cowards.

But here's the thing. It's not only almost impossible to avoid a scene, but the things that we do to avoid a scene usually just make things worse in the long run.

Take the classic idea of breaking up with someone in a crowded, fancy restaurant. *Who's going to take a nut there?* we think. But when you do that, all that's happened is that on top of whatever hurt and anger goes with the breakup, you've just added more fuel to the other person's anger, because, come on, they know that you've set things up so you won't have to hear how they feel.

You might have won round one, but round two is waiting for you around the corner, and there's an even bigger scene contained in it.

The truth is—and you should probably file this under "paradox-ical but true"—that the best, in fact the *only*, way to minimize the yelling and crying that come with a breakup is to welcome it. That's right. Break up with someone when there's plenty of time and privacy for all the emotions to come out. And you should positively elicit those emotions. Say, "I know you have a lot of feelings and a lot of things to tell me. I don't want to stop you. Let me hear everything you have to say. Let's get it all out."

You can't prevent a scene, but that's the best way to minimize how bad a scene it is.

Here's the rule of thumb. The more you welcome the other person's feelings, the more that person feels that she doesn't have to crank up her feelings to break through your resistance to them.

And to make this as painless as possible, try as much as you can to validate what the other person says. For example, if the other person says "You never wanted this relationship to succeed. You never really tried," you could say "Maybe you're right. Maybe I always held something back. I know I probably could have done more and given more." And isn't that true? It's true of almost all of us.

And please refrain from saying anything like "Yeah, but you held back even more than I did," or "Well, you sure didn't hold back—you were obsessive and smothering and overinvolved." Even if some of it might be true, by turning this into a debate over who did the most to kick the crap out of this relationship, you're just setting up a more harrowing scene.

So don't attack. Don't blame. Don't defend yourself, either. Just let all of the other person's feelings come out and validate them whenever possible.

This way the scene will burn itself out faster than any other way. You've not added any fuel to the fire.

NUTS AND MONSTERS

There's one big exception to all of this. How do you break up with someone who is crazy or evil or both? No, this doesn't refer to someone you're just mad at. I'm talking about bunny boilers, control freaks, rageaholics, and others like these. In other words, I'm talking about people who might hurt you. Maybe not physically, necessarily, but emotionally and practically.

The first rule of thumb is that you have to make a clear decision about whether the person you want to break up with falls into this category or not. No one can tell you where to draw the line. Just being a difficult or emotional person doesn't put someone in this category. They are in this category because you have evidence from the past that when you thwart them, they take things to a whole other level, where you've been really hurt or scared. If you feel that there's a good chance that they're in this category, then they're in this category. This is not one of those places where denial is your friend.

The second rule of thumb is that there's a safety-first procedure you have to follow with someone like this.

The first step in this safety-first procedure is to get the important people on board.

You need a lawyer who can advise you. You might have far more rights and options than you imagine. In addition, your lawyer can warn you against making specific mistakes. With your lawyer, you can work out a plan for what to do and when to do it.

You also need a close friend or family member who knows how to keep her mouth shut. This friend can help in 101 ways—from giving you advice and support to giving you a place to stay temporarily, and everything in between. This person also can send and receive letters and messages for you so that your plans are kept secret.

And, where necessary, you need a person who can lend or give you some money to pay a few bills and get you through the transition to being safely on your own.

If this doesn't seem doable, you have a fallback. Before you act, contact a shelter for people who are leaving abusive relationships.

The people running this shelter can advise you on what your best courses of action are, and they might be able to help you find alternatives to going to a shelter.

Once you have your people in place, start making your plan. That's the second step. You need a place to go where you and your children will be safe and have money to tide you over in a separate, secret account.

You should also get legal advice before you pull the trigger on the breakup, especially when there are kids involved. You need to find out what your rights and obligations are. In some cases, for example, you might be much better off getting a restraining order and staying in your house or apartment. Only a lawyer can advise you on these kinds of things.

Now this is most important. However tough things are, and they can be really tough, you can't tip your hand to your spouse, or to anyone who might tell your spouse. You have to play it cool until your plan and everything you need to carry it out are in place.

Step three. Do *not* have a breakup scene. Leave a letter where the other person will find it, and just don't be there when they come back. Don't confront someone who you feel is in any way dangerous.

If you follow this safety-first procedure, you and your kids will be under a new roof before your controlling spouse even knows what's going on—but he won't know your address. You'll have done the best thing to start a new, safer, and happier life.

THE ULTIMATE THREAT

There's one special issue I have to bring up because it's rather common, even though it might seem extreme. Sometimes when we break up with someone they threaten to kill themselves if we go through with it. Sometimes you've already been told "If you ever break up with me, I'll kill myself."

What do you do when you're threatened with suicide?

This is delicate, and sometimes heart-wrenching, but it's not complicated. The fact that someone threatens suicide—that they are the *kind* of person who *would* threaten suicide—is a very strong reason *not* to be in a relationship with them. It should loosen, not tighten, your bonds.

So whatever you do, don't stay with someone if they've threatened suicide. Instead, you need to make a judgment call. Is this "just a threat," or is it a real possibility? Now this is tough, because even experienced clinicians can struggle over which it is. But here is what you should do: Always assume that there is a real possibility of suicide unless you're *convinced* it's just a threat.

And if there is a real possibility, then what you've got is a psychiatric emergency. Literally. This means that you need to talk to a psychiatrist about this person being a real danger to themselves. Then follow the psychiatrist's guidance. Someone who is a real danger to themselves can be and should be subject to mandatory hospitalization for observation and treatment.

The psychiatrist might have useful ideas about the timing and procedure for you to follow in breaking up with this person. But make no mistake. *You can't let their threats, however real, trap you into a relationship that's not good for you.* This might sound cruel and cold, but you have to live the best life you can, and if someone is determined to kill themselves because you want to be happy, then you have a responsibility to help prevent them from making that choice. But you *don't* have a responsibility to sacrifice your own life. What are you going to do, spend the rest of your life with someone you don't want to be with just because they're, in effect, a mental patient?

Now what if you think the other person is just threatening suicide? Don't let them play that game. Tell them simply, "I've got to do what I've got to do, and you've got to do what you've got to do." In other words, you give their threat no power. And if you can't bring yourself to do this, then you're saying that this threat is very real and you have to treat it as a psychiatric emergency.

Those are the two choices: empty threat or psychiatric emergency. They have to be handled very differently. But in either case, you can't be with this person.

. . .

Things usually don't get this extreme. Breakups are most often scarier to contemplate than they are to live through. And being clear about wanting to break up is what will ultimately make the breakup go as smoothly as possible.

[14]

LOOK BEFORE YOU LEAP

Most of us were forced to read an O. Henry story in high school. These always featured a surprise ending. One of his best-known stories is about a young married couple who are broke. His prized possession is a pocket watch. Hers is her long, luxurious chestnut hair. In the story they are each struggling to figure out what to get the other for Christmas. She decides to surprise him by getting him a chain for his pocket watch. He decides to surprise her by getting her tortoiseshell combs for her hair.

But the real surprise, for them, and for us, comes when they realize on Christmas morning that he'd sold his watch to buy her hair combs, and she'd sold her hair to buy his watch chain. A bittersweet ending at best.

See? That's what you get when you don't talk to your partner and check things out carefully.

But you can prevent that from happening in your situation. The rule of thumb here is clear. Look before you leap. But do more than look. Check out carefully what you're leaping into, even if it's a relationship you've been in for a long time. You never know. So to carry out this guideline, *you have to talk to the person you're thinking of choosing and get some solid answers.*

But answers to what questions? What are you looking for?

DAVID'S STORY

David, 43, was the last guy in the world you'd think would be in two relationships. Hardly a suave juggler of women, David was a normally careful CPA who specialized in defending professionals charged for income-tax evasion. He was certainly someone who had a front-row seat on the dangers of being a careless screwup.

After he divorced his first wife, David was unattached for a couple of years, never doing more than going out for a casual date. Then he met Molly. Molly represented everything warm, comfortable, and supportive that David needed so much and had never gotten in his marriage. As sheer icing on the cake, David had met Molly through her work as an IRS administrator, and so they had lots in common professionally.

There was just one problem. David was a guy who loved physical activity—cycling, rock climbing, skiing, sailing—and he never enjoyed just sitting around, which is exactly what Molly enjoyed most. And there was something motherly about Molly that was comforting, but it also meant that being with her wasn't challenging for David. So while she was great, he felt she was also maybe just a little boring.

After being a couple for two years, David and Molly decided that they'd cool things for a while. Molly knew about David's restlessness and wanted to preempt being dumped. She was hoping he'd miss her and come back to her.

Well, he did miss her, and he did come back to her, but not before he got involved with Suki. What a contrast, compared to Molly. Suki was a firecracker. In a very unmotherly way, Suki challenged David at every step—his opinions, attitudes, beliefs, decisions. And he loved it. He felt so alive with her. Even better, Suki liked many of the same physical activities that he liked. Finally he had a partner when he wanted to go do something.

But strangely enough, as exciting and fun as Suki was, she made David miss Molly. Sex wasn't as good with Suki as it was with Molly. And he missed that wonderful feeling of being taken care of.

And that's when things started feeling dangerous, and not in a good way. Both women knew the other existed, but neither woman knew, as far as David could tell, the extent of his relationship with the other. So David, with the agony of a prudent man living a dangerous life, knew that the knife was at his throat, and that he'd better make a decision fast about who he wanted to be with.

It was hard, because they were both good women whom he truly cared about. In the end, David realized that it wasn't about them; it was about him. As terrific as Molly was, he didn't like his view of himself as a person choosing to be with someone because she was safe and comfortable. But he liked the sense of himself choosing to ride a tiger like Suki.

So, being responsible, he broke up with Molly and told Suki that he wanted to commit to her. This was great for a while. But then he realized that he'd made a terrible mistake. Suki liked David as a boyfriend, but either she had no desire to settle down or she had no desire to settle down with him. Maybe the main reason that she'd been so free and easy was that she just didn't care if they lasted. When she saw David getting serious, she got scared.

David, who'd started out with two great women, ended up with no one.

And all this could have been prevented if, before he hopped on the Suki bandwagon and knocked over Molly's, David had just kicked the tires a little.

So how do you go about having that serious talk with the person you're leaning toward, the talk David should have had with Suki?

JUST A LITTLE TALK

The first rule of thumb is that you should *never,* EVER frame the talk as "I'm thinking of making a commitment to you, but before I do, I'd just like to clear up a few things." I can't tell you how badly it's likely to go if you do this.

Instead, in your own words, just say something like "I'd like us to have a talk about our relationship, just to check out where we're at with each other and where we want to go. I've got some questions, and I bet you do, too." Make sure you choose a time when the two of you can really talk without interruption.

But what do you ask? The second rule of thumb is that, before you have this little talk, you should take some time and put some notes down in three categories.

ASSUMPTIONS. What is it that you're assuming is true if you go forward with this person? David assumed that Suki would want to marry him if he wanted to marry her, but the opposite was true. Are you assuming that the other person will or will not want to have kids? That the other person will or will not want to move? Have you been assuming that the other person is healthy? If you're thinking of recommitting to your spouse, have you been assuming that he can change, or that he wants to change?

Whatever is important to you, you probably have assumptions about it, and you need to ask the other person directly if your assumptions are true.

You could say something like "I'd just like to make sure that we're reading off the same page." Then ask what interviewers call an open-ended question—that's a question that can't be answered with just a yes or a no. For example, "We've sort of talked about kids, but I'd really like to know how you feel about it."

NEEDS. When you think about being in a committed relationship with this person, what are the most important needs, the top three, that you're bringing to this relationship? This is a tough question, so let me help you out here.

Some of your biggest needs will come to light from what was missing from your previous or other relationships. Maybe, for instance, you like having sex very frequently, like almost every day, but you don't get that with your spouse. It seems to be a different story, though, with your lover. Whenever you get together, you have mad, passionate sex.

But is that going to last? You need to know, because this is a real need of yours. So you ask, "You know, I was wondering. How often do you like to have sex? I know we always make love when we're together, but we're not together that often. If we were together every day, would you want to make love every day or once a week, or once a month, or what?"

The point is that you need to check out with *a direct question* whether every important need you're bringing to this relationship can actually be met. And you can't avoid asking just because you're embarrassed. If you need to be with someone who's fat in the bank-account department, then you need to ask if your free-spending lover really has the bucks to back up his image.

Think of it like this. The need you have that you don't check out will turn out to be the one that doesn't get met. And you'll have no one to blame but yourself.

FEARS. A fear is just a need we have for something *not* to happen. It's usually something that's happened in the past that you don't want to have happen again.

For example, you were with someone who was sick all the time. You loved this person, but it was a terrible drag and ultimately destroyed your relationship. So now, if you're honest with yourself, you'll acknowledge that you're afraid that the person you want to be with might be someone who's sick all the time, too.

For every fear, there's a question. Of course you can't ask "Are you planning to be sick all the time?" But you can ask "This might sound weird, but we've never talked about our health. Do you ever get sick? Do you have any ongoing health issues? Are there any hereditary health problems running through your family?"

And if the other person wants to know why you're asking this, you could say "It's just important to me to know." Or, "Well, we've been getting close, and I just thought I should ask."

The key is taking your own fears seriously. The one answer that you don't want to hear is vague reassurance.

If you have a real fear, then you have a right to know why you should feel confident that this fear isn't going to be a problem if you commit to this person.

CHECK OUT YOUR SPOUSE

It's just as important to ask all these questions if the person you're thinking of committing to is the person you've already been committed to. You might think that there's no point in asking because you already know all the answers.

But you don't. Not unless you ask and push forward until you get a solid, bankable answer.

Suppose your spouse has had issues with depression. Now things seem to be better. But why are they better? And do you have a reason to think that they are going to stay better?

You have to ask. If things are better because your spouse is now on medication, that's great, but, for example, you need to know if your spouse is experiencing side effects, and how bad they are. Otherwise, by sheer coincidence, your spouse could go off the antidepressants the day you make a firm commitment to stay in the marriage.

The point is that when you're making a commitment to someone you have to check out carefully what you're getting into. I estimate that well over half of all divorces could have easily been prevented if the people had checked to see if their assumptions were warranted before they made their commitment.

LET THEM CHECK YOU OUT

It is just as important that you ask questions to determine what the *other* person's assumptions, needs, and fears are. After all, how can you be happy in this relationship if the other person is not happy? And how can they be happy if they're disappointed with what you bring to the table?

This is a conversation a lot of us tiptoe away from, because we're scared. We don't want to know what the other person is expecting and needing. It's like asking for a giant, impossible to-do list.

But the reality is usually less scary. After his wife found out about his affair—and that period in his life really was scary for both of them—Paul, 39, came to the realization that he did want to be with his wife and not his lover.

But, of course, his wife, Cami, was very hurt and angry, and so Paul was afraid that when he talked to her about moving back into the house and making a go of it, she would have an alarming list of demands. He was willing to accept purgatory but not hell.

But check out what Cami put on the table. Her main assumption was that Paul would never cheat again, or even come close, and if he did, then their marriage was over forever. Okay. Paul understood that and could live with it.

Her main need was that the two of them go into couples therapy. "Real therapy," Cami said ominously, by which Paul figured she meant talking about all the important issues. Paul's first reaction was that he'd rather have major surgery—"At least you just get that over with"—but he soon realized that therapy could actually make their relationship better, and what's more, he could bring his own issues and needs into their therapy, and that sounded great.

Cami's big fear was that she couldn't make Paul happy. Why else had he had an affair? This led to tears, and for a while both felt miserable. But then Cami had the bright idea that they'd each tell the other what each needed from the other to be happy. They drew up a list. And when they looked at the specifics, it all seemed very doable.

ONE LAST CHECK

If you're thinking of making a commitment to someone, then your life is about to turn a corner. And here I come along asking you to look around the corner that lies ahead. And I feel at a loss, because on some level you can't really teach someone how to do that. Most of us have a lot of trouble thinking about what might lie ahead—until it smacks us in the face.

So let me try to simplify it. To look before you leap and check out what you're getting into before you commit, or recommit, to someone, do this. Ask yourself one question:

What's important to you when you think about being with this person?

If something's important to you, you need to ask questions that will show you what's what about the situation.

You can't be vague. It's important to all of us that we be "happy," and that we be with someone who is "nice." But that's useless. However, if it's important to you that the other person make her obnoxious, layabout son move out of the house, which he can do, since he's 23, then *that's* something you can check out and nail down.

Remember, happiness and misery may be general kinds of feelings, but they always come from very specific, concrete causes, like from a cool breeze on a hot day or one tiny little mosquito that's found its way into your bedroom. And it's the specifics that you have to ask about.

Just think. Happiness lies so close now. All you have to do is know what's important to you, figure out what you're counting on, get specific, and ask smart questions to show you what's what.

• • •

So far we've talked about how to choose your future. Finally it's time to talk about building your future.

HEALING THE PAST, BUILDING A FUTURE

[15]

IT'S NOT ABOUT
SAYING YOU'RE SORRY

There are only two stages in a relationship. Ignorance. And rehab.
You're either in that blissful period where you don't know everything about each other, and everything is new, and most of what's
new is delightful. Or you've figured out how you've been stepping
on each other's toes, and now you're trying to repair and prevent
damage.

So, of course, almost all of us are in relationship rehab. After
all, the ignorance phase can only last a few months. It might be a
mostly contented, loving, happy rehab, but rehab it is.

I guess I'm saying this because I don't want you to feel sorry for
yourself. It always feels as if the way back is a long one, but at least
you're in excellent company with almost everyone else.

REAL HEALING

Of course there are always particular reasons for being in relationship rehab, and in your case it's because you almost certainly have some real healing to do.

If you're going back to a spouse who knows about your affair, it's obvious that healing has to happen.

If you're committing to your lover, that might sound like a happy ending, but you'd be making a big mistake if you thought that your lover did not have trust issues and anger over how long it's taken you to make up your damned mind to get out of your marriage.

And even if you're committing to a spouse who doesn't know about your affair, you don't get a free pass. There clearly have been some things missing in your marriage, and a lot of frayed edges, and neither of you will be happy if you don't do some work on it.

The healing you need to do requires three main ingredients.

You need to deal with the other person's pain—her anger, her hurt, her loss of self-esteem.

You need to rebuild trust.

And you need to make the other person feel loved.

It sounds like work, and it is. But it's the best work in the world, because it's the only work that produces both joy and intimacy.

In this chapter, we're going to deal with the first ingredient in relationship rehab.

PAIN MANAGEMENT

How do you deal with someone who's in emotional pain? Especially when it's pain you're largely responsible for?

Brian, 54, was a program manager for a popular local FM music station. He was one of those guys who are efficient at work and chaotic in their personal lives. His wife, Betty, whom he'd been with since college, picked up all the slack. You can be someone's lover, or you can be someone's manager, but it's extremely difficult to be both at the same time. As the years went by, Betty the manager displaced Betty the lover. Things went as smoothly as they could, given Brian's penchant for chaos. But it was a smoothness slowly stripped of love.

Feeling very guilty for his lack of loyalty, Brian nonetheless had a series of affairs. They meant nothing to him. Looking for love, he found only sex.

Then he met Claire. This was a relationship with more substance. He could talk to Claire, and he enjoyed doing so.

But he surprised himself by not giving his heart to Claire. It was paradoxical. The more he learned to value Claire, the more he saw that he loved his wife. Not that it was this straightforward. It was very confusing for a long time. But eventually Brian became certain that he had to recommit to Betty.

Unfortunately, this decision came just a few days before Betty found out about Claire. Betty was devastated, and Brian was out on his ear.

But Brian broke things off with Claire completely and confessed everything to Betty. And he begged her to take him back. She agreed. But Brian was scared. Betty had been so racked by tears that she seemed shrunken, like a wet towel wrung dry.

At first Brian made the common mistake of going on and on about how sorry he was, sobbing with remorse while Betty sat there stone-faced, all cried out. Not that it was a calculated move— Brian was genuinely stricken with remorse—but still he was confused at how little impact his apologies had on Betty. Before he knew it, he found himself scolding Betty: "What's wrong with you? Can't you see how sorry I am?"

What was Brian's mistake here? Isn't it a good thing to show someone how sorry you are for hurting them?

Here's where Brian, and the millions of people like him, went wrong. Apologies are good. Remorse is appropriate. *But when you've hurt someone the way he had, being sorry makes the whole thing about your pain, not the other person's.* It's actually the easy way out.

Here's someone you've hurt. And you've hurt them in a special way—a humiliating way that makes them feel like nothing. Now they have all this emotional pain, layers of it, each layer different from the next.

And there's nothing worse than having your pain made invisible. *Healing begins when your pain is acknowledged and understood.* So for Brian to create healing, he needed to shut up about his own sorrow and really listen to Betty talk about her pain.

Most people just don't get this. For one thing, it hurts to hear someone talk about how you've hurt them. But it also seems to go against common sense. How does welcoming the other's pain make it go away?

SAVING RAPUNZEL

Your partner, yelling and crying, is really like Rapunzel letting down her hair to you and giving you a way to climb back in her good graces. You've made her feel unsafe and invisible. Her hope, and yours, is that by you being fully aware of how much and in what ways you've hurt her, you will really see her, and really seeing the damage you've done will make it vastly less likely that you will ever hurt her again like that.

So the rule of thumb here is this. The organ through which you promote healing is your ears.

It doesn't just mean listening passively and occasionally muttering "I hear you." It's more active than that. It's a real conversation. You ask questions and make comments, just the way you would in any conversation where you are really interested. But you're doing much more listening than talking, and your questions and comments aren't focused on you but on the other person. And on deepening your understanding of what she has to say.

And this is going to go on for quite a while. It's almost like a law of nature: Whenever we hurt someone, their need to talk about their pain will always go on past the point that we feel we can tolerate hearing about it.

And this is where we make another huge mistake. As the days go by, and the other person peels off yet another layer of pain and shoves it under our noses, we start saying things like "Look, I said I was sorry." Or, "Don't you think this has gone on long enough?" Or, "When are you going to get over this?"

Whether we realize it or not, what we're really doing here is trying to make it seem as though there were something wrong with the other person for being so hurt by what we did.

But here's the deal. If the other person is just some kind of a nut who wants to use her pain to make you feel guilty and control you, then you shouldn't be with her. But if this is a normal person who's been hurt, and the process is taking longer than you'd like, longer maybe than you think possible, it doesn't mean there's anything wrong with them. *This is what healing looks like.* This is the price you have to pay.

DON'T FORGET YOUR LOVER. I've focused on the hurts that come from dealing with someone who's found out that you've cheated on them. But if you commit to your lover, there are going to be hurts there, too. Don't be discouraged—most of us are in relationship rehab anyway.

So while you may think that you're running into the gleeful arms of a lover who's long been waiting for you, and now finally has you, there's pain there, too, that needs to be healed. Why did it take you so long to come around to her? Don't you realize how painful those frequently long nights were when she was all alone? Don't you understand how humiliating it all was to her?

You've got to listen to this. Sure, you need to say—and show— how sorry you are. But mostly it's about listening and showing that you truly understand the pain you've caused.

IF YOUR SPOUSE IS IN THE DARK

What if you're recommitting to a spouse who knows nothing about your recommitment because she knows nothing about your affair? Well, again, we're all in relationship rehab, maybe you a little more than most because, after all, there was something going on that led you to have an affair. And if there are ways you were hurt, there are ways your partner was hurt, because that's the way it goes in the demolition derby of love.

Here the rule of thumb is a little different. Here you need to say something like this: "You know, honey, over the years I know I've done things that have hurt you. I just want you to know how sorry I am."

But your partner probably won't say, "Oh, well, that's okay then." For the first time maybe ever, your partner will feel that there's an opening for him to talk about his pain. Which brings us right back to the first guideline: You heal with your ears, and with all the sympathy and understanding you can muster. Take full responsibility for all the things you've done wrong. Bring up your own examples of hurts you've inflicted on your spouse. But leave out the affair.

MAKING AMENDS

There's one part of healing that we haven't touched on yet. It's where you do something that your partner would experience as making amends. This is a dangerous area. When you've been hurt by someone, usually the biggest issue for you is feeling invisible, unimportant, ignored. That's what it means to be hurt. You've been treated as if you were nothing.

So if you make amends the wrong way, it can look like you're paying the other person to just shut up.

If I go into the fridge at your office where you've stowed your lunch and just take it and eat it, it doesn't help if I say "Hey, sorry." You're probably going to say "Why would you do something like that?"

You're not asking why because you're a behavioral scientist. You're asking why because you desperately want there to be some reason other than that you just don't matter. And if I say "All right, all right, here's five bucks," that's not all right, even if that was the value of your lunch, because you've still been treated like a nonentity.

And so showing that you really have heard and understand the pain you've caused is crucial. And it can be wiped out by a thoughtless, premature attempt to take away the hurt by some action. "I'm sorry I slept with your sister. Here are the keys to a brand-new Miata. Are we even now?"

Uh . . . no. Maybe a new Bentley . . . but still no. All the goodies and bling in the world won't prove that you've really understood the enormous hurt you've caused. The big gift merely says "Look, I don't really understand all the ways I've hurt you, but whatever they are, there are a lot of them, so here's a tennis bracelet. Clearly with you I can buy myself out of trouble."

And by the way, it's no more helpful if you do something to punish yourself instead of giving the other person a gift. I'm thinking of a couple who came to see me after she'd caught him cheating. I could tell very quickly that it would be very hard to save this relationship. When the woman had started telling him how hurt she was, the guy said, "Okay, I know I hurt you. I'm sorry, okay? Look, I'm going to hurt myself so we'll be even." And he picked up a Chinese back-scratcher that was lying around and started whacking himself on the head with it, hard.

That's when this woman knew it was over. He wasn't interested in her. He was interested in shutting her up.

Try to avoid making empty gestures to preempt the hard work of understanding what the other person has gone through.

But you probably have to do something. At some point, when you've listened and listened and listened, and really shown that you've heard and understood, you need to show your willingness to do something. The best question you can ask at this point is: "What do you need from me that would help?"

It's probably not going to be about you making amends. Instead, it's probably going to be about you making some sort of change, something that really indicates that you understand that it can't be business as usual. And that could be anything. You going into individual therapy. You being willing to move to a new part of the country. You selling your boat. You finally putting your foot down and not letting your mother come for monthlong visits whenever she wants.

Now here's the thing. If you really have listened and understood, you'll probably have a good sense of what the other person needs. You'll certainly have a good sense of why she needs it.

And you might be asked to make amends. If so, you're entitled to know why your partner thinks that making amends in some particular way will promote healing between you: "How does me finally cleaning out the garage help you to forgive me?"

The answer to this question will be important. It will promote more understanding between you. And that's what healing is. Two hearts knitting back together through understanding.

■ ■ ■

There's one part of healing that I haven't touched on yet. Rebuilding trust. And if there's been an affair, that's essential.

[16]

DON'T THINK TRUST,
THINK BOWLING BALLS

One of the questions I'm asked most frequently is whether you can rebuild trust once it's been damaged.

It's a good question. On a superficial level, you might think that trust can never be rebuilt. If I go to your house, and through sheer carelessness drop the incredibly valuable and much-loved china teapot that's been in your family for generations, why should you ever trust me not to do something like that again? After all, I'm the person who did it the first time. Which means that I'm the *kind* of person who *could* do it the first time. So why not the next time?

And that's the clue to how you can rebuild trust. You have to show that you're *no longer* the kind of person who would do something like whatever it was that you did.

This takes time. And it takes consistency. Rebuilding trust is like carrying a bowling ball up a flight of stairs one step at a time. If you're careless at any point and drop it, the ball will roll, *thud, thud, thud,* all the way back to the bottom. To rebuild trust you have to know what to do, and then very patiently keep doing it without screwing up.

KIM'S STORY

Kim, 42, had a big problem earning the trust of her new husband. Here's what happened. By the time Kim had been married to her first husband, Doug, for ten years, almost all the good feelings were gone. He was away traveling for work much of the time, but when he was home he was cold and verbally abusive. His main bone of contention was that Kim was a horrible, neglectful mother, which she wasn't.

But people are reluctant to divorce when they have young children. And there was more glue: Sex with Doug was great. Kim herself couldn't understand it. How could she open herself up to such a cold, hostile man? Their sexual chemistry was just great, though, and Doug could be charming when he wanted to be. Their sex was almost always makeup sex.

Kim fell for Sean the first time she met him, when they were both picking up their kids from school. Sean was recently divorced. They instantly hit it off. He had the sweet, rumpled, casual, earthy quality of a guy who'd been an English major at an Ivy League college but who went on to become a high-end furniture maker. The over-the-top sexual chemistry wasn't there for Kim with Sean, but sex was okay, and in every other way they got along great. Sean made Kim feel loved and happy.

After Kim and Sean had said they loved each other, it took Kim a year and a half to tell Doug that she wanted a divorce. That year and a half was hell for Sean. He couldn't understand why it was taking Kim so long to announce to Doug what she'd declared to Sean.

To make matters worse, Sean had somehow gotten the impression that Kim hadn't been sleeping with Doug anymore, that things had gotten so bad that that part of their relationship was over. So imagine how Sean's jaw hit the floor when Kim casually mentioned one day that "of course" she was still sleeping with Doug.

Sean said, "You tell me that you're a few weeks away from getting Doug to move out and you're still sleeping with him!?! No! I don't want you sleeping with him anymore. How do you think it makes me feel?"

But Kim hesitated, making it sound as though it would be somehow "weird" if she stopped sleeping with him, and so Sean pushed. The more Sean pushed, the less Kim could think of to say, until finally she told the truth, which was how great sex with Doug was.

If someone's head could explode, Sean's would have gone bang. He felt totally betrayed, but the mind-blowing twist was that Kim was cheating on her lover with her husband. Sean couldn't wrap his mind around the complexity of it.

This almost blew Kim's relationship with Sean out of the water. Kim saved things by moving fast to get Doug out of her house, and to proceed as fast as possible toward a divorce. She didn't push for a large cash settlement, just for joint custody. Soon her house was sold, she was living with Sean, and before long they were married.

But Sean had a hard time trusting Kim, and this soon started to eat away at their new marriage. Kim had made a big deal to Sean about how for the sake of their kids she wanted them to see that she and their dad got along. So she'd spend time at Doug's house, supposedly with the kids, but Sean could never be sure.

Finally, Sean got Kim to agree that her kids didn't need to see her hanging out with their dad to feel safe. Kim agreed not to spend any more time with Doug.

And it was with that that trust had a chance to begin to heal. That was when Kim could start carrying the bowling ball of healing up the stairs slowly and carefully, one step at a time. All she had to do was completely end things with Doug.

And then Sean would have been able to trust Kim. Yes, rebuilding trust happens slowly at first, like the first few months of learning to play the piano. But then trust starts picking up steam, and there's that magic moment when it returns. You can never capture this one, just the way you can never capture the one when a headache goes away, but it's there.

And it would have been there for Sean and Kim if he hadn't seen a new e-mail in which Kim mentioned to Doug that she really enjoyed their last time together. Thud, thud, thud, the bowling ball of trust rolled all the way back to the bottom. Kim swore up and down that this was only about a brief chat she'd had with Doug the last time she'd picked up her kids. But it didn't matter. It was too late. The damage was done.

It's often hard to tell if the possibility of trust is dead. What you can be sure of is that every time the bowling ball gets dropped and falls to the bottom, the next time the stairs are a lot steeper, and it's harder to bring it all the way to the now further-away top without a mishap.

That's where Kim and Sean are now. No one is perfect, but Kim knows that if she's going to make it with Sean, her only hope is being perfect in not doing anything further to erode Sean's trust.

ONE STEP AT A TIME

Reestablishing trust is actually easier than I'm making it sound, and the reason is clarity. As long as you and the other person have gotten clarity between you about what you need to do, or not do, to rebuild trust, then the path ahead of you is well marked.

Just make sure you do, or don't do, what you've agreed on. All Kim had to do was not spend time in person with Doug, who was a known sex magnet.

And what is it *you* need to do? Talk to your partner. For example:

"I don't want you to have anything more to do with that woman." That's clear. This means no phone calls, no e-mails, no chats over coffee. This means "nothing."

Now you might say "Okay, but the person I was having an affair with is someone in my office whom I see every day. I can't refuse to interact." The key is talking to your partner about this and hoping that he's not so badly hurt that he can't be reasonable. But be prepared for your partner to say that you need to look for a new job.

This is when we're tempted to blow up and accuse the other person of being paranoid. But that's probably not fair. You're judging yourself by your intentions. And you may very well firmly intend to never do anything hurtful again. But our intentions are always invisible to other people. That's why our intentions, which count for so much to us, count for little to the people we're closest to.

They have only two things to go by: the past and the future. And, based on the past, you already stand condemned. After all, you've done something to hurt their trust. So all you have to work with is the future, *your actions* in the future. And don't neglect the obvious: Make it totally clear that you will never, ever even come close to cheating again.

If the person with whom you're trying to rebuild trust is a nut, then you shouldn't be with him. A nut, in this case, is someone who is in love with his own paranoia. Or it's someone who is thrilled to have this opportunity to control you. Does that describe your partner? If not, then he's not a nut; he's just someone who's really hurt and scared. And all that means is that you have your work cut out for you.

A SHORTCUT

Are there shortcuts in the trust-building process? *Yes.* The key is that you can't be a reluctant trust builder. The shortcuts develop when you become eager, proactive. To do this you need to seek out ways to sacrifice your comfort and freedom in the short run for the sake of your partner's happiness and peace of mind in the long run.

In other words, offer to do things your partner might not have thought of or might not have wanted to ask for. For example, you could ask if it would help if you called every hour to check in, at least for the near future. Would it help if you gave your partner the password to your computer so she could check on your e-mails?

We naturally resent having to do things like this. But remember, you're judging yourself by your intentions, but you're being judged—and can only be judged—by your actions. The best way to deal with your resentment is to decide if your partner is a nut and, if not, to accept that this is the smart way to create a shortcut to rebuilding trust.

LISTENING

There is one other dimension to regaining your partner's trust, and it's the very same thing that you did to heal the hurts. It requires listening. You need to listen as your partner unpacks all the ways you've hurt her. This is essential for regaining trust. How can she feel safe unless she knows you really, *really*, REALLY have seen the full impact of what you've done?

Jason, 55, was head of a sports-marketing firm. After fifteen years helping him develop the business, his wife, Angela, 51, went to school to study filmmaking. Then she discovered that he'd just ended a brief affair with a woman in their circle. He wasn't surprised that Angela was upset, but he thought he could alleviate her suffering by pointing out that this woman didn't really mean anything to him.

A million cheaters have said this, and a million spouses have responded the way Angela did: "So you've caused all this pain and jeopardized our marriage over someone you didn't even care about! Are you evil or just stupid?"

And that's when Jason learned that to bring back trust you've got to explore a very complex geography of suffering. For example, having forced Jason to reveal every detail of his brief, stupid affair, Angela found herself oppressed by the knowledge of all the places near where they live and work that Jason had spent time with this woman, or where this woman would hang out.

And so in this case there was a quite real geography of suffering. All the little trips Angela made to this or that store meant that over and over she'd come down the road and suddenly find herself confronted with a reminder of pain: "Oh yeah, this is where they . . ."

To live her life was, literally, painful.

Then there was Angela's body, something else that had been betrayed, another casualty of his betrayal. Aging is tough on the way we feel about our bodies. The fact that Jason would cheat on her meant, to Angela, that her body was being rejected. And that hurt. And it was hard for her not to blame her own body for his rejection. And so she lost any sense of being at peace with her body.

How could Angela trust that Jason *got it* unless she knew that he really saw all of this and was hit by the full impact of it on her?

NO SHORT CIRCUITS

The process of hearing all this will bring back trust, but there is a side effect that has to be understood and dealt with. It's a way you can get enormously confused and end up sabotaging the very thing you're trying to make happen. Here's how it works.

There you are, feeling so guilty because you've hurt someone you care about. The one thing you'd like most is to be relieved of your guilt. Having confessed your affair, you'd love it if your partner said, "Oh, that's okay. I don't blame you. I understand."

Of course in the entire history of the world this has never happened. So if you have any wisdom at all, to rebuild trust you put yourself through the ordeal of listening to all the ways the other person has been hurt by you. Now, this is no academic discussion. It happens with tears and anger. It's harrowing. It makes you feel as if you're both being torn apart. *It doesn't feel like healing*.

And so your every instinct is to put an end to this painful process. How do you heal something by ripping it to shreds?

And that's where almost everyone makes the terrible mistake. At some point you say something like "Look, haven't we gone over this a million times? Enough already. I get it—this was horrible for you—I really get it, but now I think that you're just trying to hurt me back."

This is a mistake, because it says as plain as day "Sorry, honey, but your pain, however bad, isn't as much of a big deal to me as my own discomfort." And guess what you've just conveyed? The mind-set of someone who can't be trusted. You can't trust someone who puts your hurt at a much lower value than his own discomfort.

And that's why to rebuild trust you can't short-circuit the process of listening to your partner's pain. Think of it like this. You have to dig a hole in the ground. A very deep hole. And so there's nothing for you to do but keep digging until you get all the dirt out. It's difficult. Real labor. But you can't stop until you're done. The thing is that when you're done, you've really cleared the way for trust to grow back with deeper roots than ever.

■ ■ ■

There are two parts to healing. One is getting rid of the bad stuff. We've just dealt with that by focusing on dealing with the hurts and rebuilding trust. The other part is bringing back the good stuff. That's what we're going to deal with next.

[17]

"SWEETIE, IT'S YOU"

I often ask couples who work with me to write down, on a scale from 1 to 10, how much they love their partner and how much they feel loved by their partner.

It rarely fails: People almost always feel they love their partner more than they feel loved. "I love him a nine and a half. I feel he loves me a five." Something like that.

It's true in my marriage. I know my husband would say that he loves me at a level 10. But I rarely feel loved by him quite at this level. And I'm sure my husband would say the same thing about me.

What's going on? In most marriages, if love were a pipeline, it would be in serious need of the Roto-Rooter Man, because whatever we're putting into the system, not enough is getting through.

It's that much worse in relationships that have been affected by someone having an affair. An affair is like an open wound. All three people are bleeding, sometimes more than they realize. And that includes the spouse, even if she doesn't know about the affair. No one's getting the attention they deserve. Everyone's anxious. Everyone's holding back on what they have to give. Real love, the kind that gets through the pipeline, is in short supply.

Then the affair ends. The bleeding stops. But the pipeline doesn't automatically open up. Just think about how you got here. If you're recommitting to your spouse, then at a minimum you're recommitting to someone who's been seriously deprived of all you have to offer. If you're committing to your lover, then you're committing to someone who for too long has had to share you with someone else.

There's a love shortage!

And you've got to start fixing it fast. Just think about it. There's another pipeline that causes trouble when it gets blocked. Your coronary arteries. And when that happens, it's called a heart attack. Relationships have heart attacks, too, and with just as damaging results. And they happen because not enough love is getting through.

THE DOMINO'S THEORY

The most important thing for you to get into your head is that you need to forget about the vast, warm, effervescent supply of love you know you have inside you. That's nice, but what *stays* inside you is not going to help very much. In love land, you don't get any credit for it, any more than in pizza land Domino's gets credit for the delicious pizzas it fails to deliver.

So how do you make sure your love gets through to the person you're committing to, and his love gets through to you?

It's easier than you might think.

Here's the concept. Suppose you're craving, *dying* for some cool, fresh slices of watermelon. It's spring, and you haven't had any since last summer. But all someone has to offer you is cheese puffs, which you've been eating all winter. How many cheese puffs would you have to eat to feel as satisfied as you would by one nice slice of watermelon?

A lot. In fact, you could eat cheese puffs all day long and never really feel satisfied. It's the watermelon you want.

This kind of thing goes on in love land all the time. There are things both of you need to feel loved. Everything else, *however nice,* won't make you feel loved.

Steve, 43, had had a classic see-if affair with a woman at his health club. Things had been rocky for a while between him and his wife, Melissa, 37. Nothing huge, just the distance and irritation that grow out of two people who lead incredibly busy lives and spend their time together doing chores, taking care of their children, and bickering over having the in-laws over yet again and whether or not to remodel the bathroom.

For quite a while Steve had seen Melissa as a nagging, constantly irritated wife, not that Steve was such a prize, either. For a brief while the woman he had an affair with was a relief from all this. But soon Steve realized that all he'd really wanted to do was see if the grass was greener on the other side, and he found out that it wasn't. If he couldn't make his wife happy, when she was the only woman in his life, how would he be able to make his lover happy as well?

And guess what? The minute things turned a little complicated with his lover, she started nagging him and getting irritated, too. Steve got the picture. He went back to his wife.

Steve learned through his work with me that people generally get the love they give. If he hadn't been getting much *from* Melissa, it was because he hadn't been giving much love *to* Melissa.

"But I always loved her," Steve said.

"How did you show it?" I asked.

Steve talked about presents he had bought her. Chores he did without being asked. How hard he worked at his job to support the family and make her proud of him.

"Has Melissa ever talked to you about what makes her feel loved?" I asked.

Steve had no idea. Melissa had complained about so many things over the previous few years that Steve couldn't hold in his head one specific thing that she wanted or cared about.

So here's the rule of thumb. I asked Steve to do what I'm asking you to do. I asked him to do the Feeling Loved exercise.

FEELING LOVED

You sit down with your chosen one and say something like "I want to know what makes you feel loved. I'm really sorry; I should know it, but I just don't. I need you to tell me. Just tell me five things that I could do to make you feel loved, whether I've ever done them or not. I'd like to know your language of love. And I'd like to do the same thing for you. How does that sound? That way we'll both know exactly what makes each other feel loved."

The first key to making this successful is being specific. A bad answer is "I feel loved when you're nice to me." It's bad because it doesn't point to any concrete action. What the hell is "nice"?

The second key to making this successful is that what you ask for is something the other person can do. A bad answer is "I'd feel loved if you made up for all the ways you've neglected me in the past." But how can anyone realistically ever do this?

A good answer might be "I feel loved when you come up to me and hug me and kiss me spontaneously, and not because you want to have sex with me." Or, "I feel loved when you talk to me in a gentle, loving way, and even if you get frustrated with me, you stay patient, and listen, and don't start getting angry."

It can be anything. Over the years I've heard people say things like "I'd feel loved if you lost your big belly," ". . . if you took the garbage out without being reminded," ". . . if you took my side when I disagree with your mother," ". . . if you initiated sex once in a while," ". . . if you went to visit my sister with me," ". . . if you listened to me when I talked about what a terrible day I'd had." You get the picture. Specific. Doable. That's what makes people feel loved.

And that's what happened with Steve and Melissa. Steve was stunned to learn that two of the things that made Melissa feel loved were when Steve smiled at her ("Really? I go around with such a serious puss when I'm with you?" "Uh, yes.") and when Steve remembered things she'd told him (". . . because it's how I know that you've listened to me, which is how I know you care about me").

But here's the amazing part. Steve had been feeling so unloved, with so little to give Melissa. But the things that she said made her feel loved weren't big ordeals to carry out. They were very doable. And Steve did them, thank God. And when Steve did them, Melissa felt loved. And soon, because she felt loved, she started acting much more loving toward Steve. And then Steve did feel loved. And he wondered why he'd ever wanted anyone else.

So you see, the Feeling Loved exercise can really be a magical way for a couple to lift themselves up by their bootstraps, to levitate themselves right out of the cold, stuck, distant place they'd been in. Only one little thing is required. Once you know what makes the other feel loved, you have to do it.

MAKING SURE IT WORKS. Because this is a real commitment, almost a second set of wedding vows, you need to talk honestly about the things on each other's lists. You can't agree to do something that you just don't know how to do.

For example, if your partner says "I'd feel loved if you didn't come home from work so tired," and you don't see how it's possible for you to do that, you have to say so. You could say "Help me out here. I'd love to do that for you. I just don't see how. Do you have any suggestions?"

This might lead to a discussion about how you take on more than your share of responsibilities at work. It might lead to a discussion about whether this was the right job for you. It might lead to the idea that you take a brief nap the minute you get home. Wherever it leads, you can have a constructive conversation about what you can do to make your chosen one feel loved, given that she needs you to not be so tired after work.

But after you've hashed it all out, just think about what you've gotten. By knowing what makes each other feel loved, you have the key that unlocks the gates that have blocked the pipeline of love.

ONE DAY AT A TIME

There is another enormously powerful, enormously helpful tool for rebuilding love. It might sound basic, but it's anything but. It's transformative.

This tool is "daily maintenance." Here's the principle. Love grows strong and stays strong because of the things you do every day. It's like being physically fit. You can have elaborate discussions about exactly what regimen will make you fittest, but the most important thing is doing whatever you do every single day. In love, as in so many other areas of life, consistency is the key.

And just like when you were taking Spanish in high school, every day you fall behind makes it that much harder to keep going the next day.

So how do you do daily maintenance? Actually, the question should be *what* do you do, because the answer to "how" is *every day*.

To get started, here are the top ten most important things to do to maintain a good and healthy relationship:

1. *Show how much you appreciate your partner.* Do and say little things that make it clear that "I love you and I think you're great."

2. *Touch.* Every day there needs to be hugs, kisses, gentle stroking, holding hands, and, sure, throw sex into the mix. But it's not about sex every day. It is about affectionate touching every day.

3. *Say what you need.* How does this maintain love? Saying what you need allows your partner to keep the love pipeline open by doing what you need, and prevents you from feeling resentful and deprived.

4. *Listen to the other person.* Yes, maybe they repeat themselves. Maybe you're not overjoyed at what you're hearing. But in many ways listening is the single most loving and affectionate thing you can do. And not just listening, but being actively involved in what you're hearing.

5. *Be supportive.* With few exceptions, everyone is having a hard time. Everyone's life is tough. Everyone needs help and encouragement. That means your partner needs this. And it's not just words. It means making food, rubbing shoulders, giving the kids a bath, taking out the garbage without being asked.

6. *Spend time together.* You should spend at least ten minutes every day where it's just the two of you, and you're focused on each other, and you're not talking about problems and chores and responsibilities. You're just there for each other and with each other.

7. *Have fun with each other.* Whatever fun is for you. Do something that's just a little fun every day, and something that's a lot of fun every week.

8. *Be positive.* We all go through our lives vulnerable to frustration and discouragement. So when you're negative, your partner just wants to get away from you. If you say something positive, hopeful, forward-looking every day, your partner will want to be with you.

9. *Put yourself in your partner's shoes.* Even if it's just a minute, spend some time every day thinking about what it's like to be your partner, living her life, being in a relationship with you. And if you think about this, it's got to have an effect.

10. *Be open.* Intimacy means being close to each other. How can you do that unless you show what's inside of you?

Now for the cool part. I'll bet you thought "Sounds great, but it's too much for me." Welcome to the club. We're all running on empty these days. We're all struggling with the question "How do you give when you don't feel you have anything to give?"

The answer is that you focus your energy on what gives you the most leverage. Show your partner this list of items of daily maintenance. Ask her which *three* items she feels you've been neglecting the most. I know—she'll probably say that you've been neglecting all of them. That's the way it is these days. So you have to say "Yeah, I know, but just as a start, which three have I been neglecting *most?*"

And that's what you focus on for the next three months, those three, not all ten. See? I told you it would be easier than you thought.

And that's really all you have to do to bring back your love:

- Do those things that make your chosen one feel loved.
- Every day do the three items of daily maintenance that you've both been neglecting the most.

It's not magic. But before you know it, it brings the magic back.

EXING OUT YOUR EX

And to keep your love growing, remember to keep the "ex" in your ex. Your former relationship is over. Whether it's your ex-spouse or your ex-lover, there shouldn't be any phone calls, lunches, e-mails, *nothing*. You shouldn't even talk *about* your ex. It should be as though that person never existed. That's because every time your ex's name reappears in your life, it sets your chosen one's healing back a couple of months. Your ex is a nonperson as far as you being busy with your ex is concerned.

There are two huge exceptions to this.

If your partner wants to talk about your ex, then open up.

And if you and your ex have children together, then of course your ex is going to come up. But even then, your conversation should be limited to logistics: "My ex wants me to pick the kids up early this weekend. Is that okay with you?"

. . .

They say relationships take work. I've never liked that idea. It turns love into a chore. What I've been talking about in this chapter has nothing to do with work. Instead, it's just about being thoughtful, caring, and consistent. It's just about doing what you know will be effective.

And if you do that, there's nothing to prevent the love in your life from growing strong forever.

[18]

THE LOVE YOU'VE
BEEN SEARCHING FOR

Well, you've come a long way. You started out in a terrible mess, utterly confused, at risk of losing everything you care about.

And now you see a way to come home, wherever home for
your heart happens to be. There is someone who's right for you.
There is a way to sort things out. There is a way for you to find happiness.

But the treasure map isn't the treasure. I've shown you the way.
You have to make the journey.

You have a lot to think about. But you're not alone anymore.
And you can keep referring to what you've read as often as you
need to. This will get you where you want to go, and this path, the
right path, is a lot easier, and a lot safer, than where you've been.

It all began with your search for real love, and you deserve to
find it. And it's there, waiting for you to make it happen.

Do you have any questions for me? Comments? Do you need
further help? Then please visit me at www.mirakirshenbaum.com.
I'd love to hear from you.

STUFF YOU
NEED TO
KNOW ABOUT
DIVORCE

LAWYERS AND MONEY: OUCH!

This is not a book about divorce. It's about getting yourself out of the mess of being in two relationships and putting your love life back in order. Of course, for many people doing that will mean getting divorced.

First, they need to know how to act effectively.

Second, they need to see what's involved, because sometimes that changes their decision to get divorced in the first place.

To help with this, in this resource section I'm going to tackle two topics. First, I'm going to explore the issues of lawyers and money. Then I will tackle the issue of helping children deal with divorce.

ONCE UPON A TIME

Let me tell you a fable. Once upon a time, there was a woman named Lisa, 33, who was walking down a long, muddy, difficult path. Every step was labored, and it seemed without end. Lisa was terribly discouraged. Day after day she slogged along the path. Then, one morning, she passed an elf sitting on a log.

"Look," he said, pulling aside a bush, "here's the entrance to an underground passage. Why not go into this? It will take you off this terrible path you've been stuck on. And who knows, maybe it will lead you to someplace much better."

"Will it?" Lisa said.

"Yes," said the elf, "maybe. If you don't get lost. And if you don't make any wrong turns."

"But how can I prevent that?" Lisa asked.

"You need a guide. Someone who knows the way."

"Where can I find such a guide? Could you be that guide?"

"Yes, I could," said the elf, "and my fee is only five hundred dollars an hour."

"But can I trust you?" Lisa said.

"For the kind of money you'd be paying me, I sure hope so."

This is actually a true story. Minus the elf and the underground passage, of course. Lisa had been married for seven years to a very controlling guy. They had three children. Life with Eric wasn't hell. He didn't abuse her in any overt way. It's just that Lisa felt that Eric had pulled a horrid switcheroo on her. He'd pursued her, and said he loved her, but no sooner had they gotten married than Lisa felt it was very clear that Eric just wanted a pretty wife, someone to have sex with, and a mother for the children they would have. He didn't love Lisa or care about her.

Now you might think that it's hard to have an affair when you're a stay-at-home mom with three little kids, and it is. But it's not impossible. Especially not for Lisa when Bobby came back into her life. He'd been Lisa's boyfriend in high school. They'd drifted apart when Lisa went off to college.

One day they happened to run into each other at Home Depot. Even though it had been years since they'd last seen each other, they had one of those relationships where the connection never quite went away. Instead of going to Starbucks, they went to sit in Bobby's car to talk.

Within minutes Lisa burst into tears, telling Bobby how difficult her life was now.

Within a month they were having a full-blown affair, aided by unknowing friends and relatives who babysat the kids while Lisa went out to do "errands."

Six months later, partly because of guilt but more because she was in sheer hell, Lisa felt that she had to break things off with Bobby. She knew their affair would be discovered sooner or later if she kept it up. She didn't see how she could divorce her husband, even though she wanted to, because he had all the cards. It wasn't just that she had no money. It wasn't just that she suspected he knew about her affair anyway. There was also the fact that over the course of their marriage Lisa had now and then consulted a psychiatrist about her anxiety and depression, and her husband was the kind of guy who would try to use this against her.

Lisa was afraid that she'd lose her kids and have no money.

"Why not talk to a lawyer?" Bobby said one day. "I know a guy . . ."

But Lisa felt too vulnerable to consult a lawyer. Think of that lawyer as the elf. And think of the world he would lead her into as a dark, scary underground passage. Better, she thought, to stay on the painful, difficult path she knew. Bye-bye Bobby. Bye-bye happiness.

This is how many of us feel when we start thinking about the practicalities of getting a divorce. There it is, hope of escape just out of reach, but it feels too overwhelming to make it happen.

We're afraid of losing our kids. We're afraid of a punitive, impoverishing financial settlement. We're afraid of being alone. And we're afraid that the price of this "bargain" is buying some lawyer a boat.

So how do you handle this scary, confusing moment in the path of your life?

HANDLING LAWYERS

Here are the rules of thumb. Pay attention. They could make all the difference.

The first rule of thumb is that, in spite of your fear of scary elves, you need to talk to a lawyer not only before you break up but *before you make your final decision about whether to break up.*

Here's the thing. You probably have rights you don't even know about, but you may also have obligations you don't realize. Not only that, but your spouse probably has obligations you've not been aware of. More ominous, he may have rights you haven't considered as well.

All this adds up to the first thing you need to learn from your lawyer. Ask the lawyer: *"After all the negotiating is over, and after we appear before the judge, what is the most likely settlement I'll be looking at, particularly looking at child custody and at money?"* Until you get an answer to this question, you can't possibly be thinking intelligently about whether to break up or not.

It's this likely settlement, not some fantasy about breaking free or being cast aside, that you're choosing when you opt for divorce. That's why you've got to know what this likely settlement looks like.

That brings us to the next rule of thumb.

Good lawyers are out there. Unfortunately, they look exactly like bad lawyers. You can't tell them apart. They don't come labeled good or bad in the yellow pages. The size of their fee or the prestige of the law firm they work for are not indicators of how good they are. But someone else can point you to a good lawyer, someone who's had a good experience himself with that lawyer.

So you need to talk to people. Best are people who've recently been divorced themselves. Ask them three questions: *"Did you like your lawyer? Was he/she easy to work with? Did he/she do a good job for you?"* A *yes* answer to all three questions is a very good sign.

If you can't ask people who've recently been divorced, ask professionals you know, your doctor, your clergy, your accountant. If they say that so-and-so is good, you must ask *"How do you know?"* Yes, it's a slightly rude question, but this is your life. What you want to hear is that this professional has direct experience of how this lawyer has done a good job for people.

Asking around like this is hard for some people. You might live in a community where everyone knows everyone else's business. You don't want it to come out that you're looking for a lawyer. But maybe there are still people you can trust to keep their mouths shut.

If none of these sources of referrals works for you, you still have a good option. In most parts of the country, there's a state or city bar association that has a free referral service. You call up and say you're looking for a divorce lawyer, and they will give you the name of a lawyer who will talk to you for free for thirty minutes.

This is a good deal! In thirty minutes you can get a lot of your questions answered. But be a good shopper. *Does the lawyer seem interested in you? Does he answer your questions in a direct and understandable way? Does she seem helpful? Does he seem organized and efficient? Does it seem as though she has a well-run office?*

But don't stop there. Call the bar association's referral service back and get the name of a second lawyer (they sometimes restrict themselves to one referral at a time). Talk to this lawyer. And then call the association and get the name of a third person.

The reason you need to talk to three lawyers is that you'll learn a lot about your case, plus there's no other way to size up any one lawyer except by comparison. The first person you talked to, who seemed okay, might seem like a dud after the third lawyer. But three should be enough.

Here's the point. If you go about your search for a lawyer carefully, in any of the ways I've just outlined, then you've greatly increased your chances of finding a lawyer who will do a good job for you.

Before you hire a lawyer, there are some things you need to get clear about. You need to know how much he charges and what exact services he charges for. For example, if you call him up with a quick question, is there a charge for that? How much? Get it all clear up front.

And there's something else. You need to be clear that the lawyer sees you as a full partner in this process. One of the biggest complaints people have about lawyers is that they are treated in a paternalistic way, "managed" rather than being provided full information. This is not good. You need a lawyer who will talk to you about what he's doing and why he's doing it, and who will continually tell you what your options are and the pros and cons of each.

FIRING LAWYERS

We're already talking about the next rule of thumb, which has to do with the nature of your relationship with the lawyer. Here's where people get into trouble. They confuse trusting someone with giving power over to that person. Okay, you don't hire a lawyer you can't trust. But never forget that he or she works for *you*. And people who work for you can be fired if you don't like the job they're doing.

But before you fire your lawyer, talk to him. Explain why you're not happy. One guy I interviewed for this book told me, "I was starting to get madder and madder at my lawyer. He was calling me with a million questions, and I was getting charged for every little call. It was weird, like I had to hold his hand or something. I almost fired him, but I decided to talk to him first. It turns out—and I remember this—that when we first met I said something about my being a kind of hands-on, control-freak kind of guy. I was totally exaggerating. I just wanted him to know he couldn't run roughshod over me. It never occurred to me that he'd take it in the direction that he did. We were both relieved after our little chat, and things were fine after that."

So think of your lawyer as someone you're dating, not someone you're married to. (Of course, it's not a great idea to *actually* date your lawyer, particularly while she's representing you!) She's your lawyer until she stops working out, and then you get another lawyer. It's a terrible mistake to fall into the mind-set that the worst catastrophe would be to have to start all over with another lawyer. You wouldn't have to start all over. The second lawyer would pick up where the first left off.

The worst catastrophe is allowing your divorce to go to settlement or to judgment while you're represented by an untrustworthy or incompetent lawyer.

Remember the elf and the underground passage? Well, if you follow these guidelines, you'll be in a very different place. Instead of a creepy and mysterious elf, you'll have a lawyer you can relate to and trust. Instead of a dark and dangerous passage, you'll be going down a path where you have a clear sense of what's happening at each step and how things are most likely to turn out.

WHEN IT *IS* ABOUT THE MONEY

As long as we're talking about lawyers, we might as well talk about money.

Money is dangerous. When people are upset, they make stupid

decisions about money. And thinking about money makes people upset. You can see the potential for a real vicious cycle here.

Well, I know you're upset and overwhelmed. You wouldn't be reading this book if you weren't. But still, you can take a deep breath and clear your head and try to think calmly about money.

A divorce is something you buy, just like anything else. And like anything you buy, it's worth it at some prices and not worth it at others. One way to think about your divorce is by comparing it to hiring someone to clean out your basement. You might pay someone a few hundred bucks to do that, but it would be insane to spend tens of thousands of dollars to do it.

In the same way, it might be worth it to impoverish yourself a little for the sake of getting rid of your spouse, but you have to ask if it's worth impoverishing yourself completely. It might be, if you're in an abusive relationship and there's literally no alternative other than stealing away in the middle of the night with just the shirt on your back.

But a lot of people get the romantic idea that they just want to be free, and damn the cost. Three years later they realize how much money they've thrown away.

So the rule of thumb here is to be very thoughtful about what you're willing to spend and what you're hoping to get for it. I'll lay it out for you.

If you spend too little—in the sense of not having a lawyer or being poorly represented, or simply in the sense of not being determined to get what's rightfully yours—you could end up with very little. Your short-term relief over getting out of your marriage could soon turn to long-term regret over what you left on the table.

If you spend too much—in the sense of an overaggressive, "I'd rather starve than see you get a dime of my money" approach—then it's very possible that no one will get anything except the lawyers.

Now you see why it's so important to have a lawyer you can

trust, who can advise you about what a realistic, reasonable settlement should look like. It's stupid to spend less than what's necessary to get that. It's stupid to spend more than that.

Ultimately, money needs to be seen in the right perspective. Always remember this rule of thumb. You're not choosing between two people. You're choosing between two ways of living, between two packages that involve people, relationships, places, pleasures, and other things. And money is an important player in this drama.

PROTECTING THE KIDS WHEN THERE'S A DIVORCE

Okay, suppose you decide that on balance it's best to end your marriage, whether or not this means making a commitment to your lover. What's the best way to handle things with your kids?

This is a huge topic, and there are some good books on the subject, some for you, some for your kids. But I've been a couples and family therapist for thirty years and I've learned a lot about what's most important when kids are involved in a divorce.

KID CONSERVATIVES

As adults, some of us are more liberal and some more conservative. But all children are conservatives in the sense that they don't typically like changes. They like their routines and find comfort in them. So as you plan for what your child's life is going to be like after you separate, try to introduce as few changes as possible.

For example, if your child can spend most nights in the house he's used to, that's a plus. If he can stay in the same school, that's a plus. You get the point.

Sometimes, of course, real shifts in patterns are necessary. Sometimes the house has to be sold and everyone must move. In a case like this, take the time to think about how a negative experience of change can be minimized.

For instance, if your kid has Scooby-Doo bedding that he really likes, get two sets, so his bed looks and feels the same at your place and your ex's. If he's used to Daddy always being the one to read him a bedtime story, then either Daddy should do it over the phone when the kid is at Mommy's house or, at a minimum, Mommy should make sure she reads him the stories he wants to hear.

GETTING TO OKAY

When a kid learns that his parents are getting a divorce, he has only one question in his mind at first: "Am I going to be okay?" Everything you say and do should be designed to help him see that he will indeed be okay.

Here are the rules of thumb for how to handle it.

BEFORE YOU AND YOUR SPOUSE TELL YOUR CHILD THAT YOU'RE GETTING A DIVORCE, WORK OUT BETWEEN THE TWO OF YOU WHAT YOUR JOINT STORY IS GOING TO BE. You need to have one explanation about why you're getting divorced that you can both agree on and stick to.

This should be a story the child can repeat to himself and to his friends. It needs to be a story a child can hold in his head, understand, and accept, so make sure it's age appropriate. Kids can deal with the fact that you don't get along anymore. They can accept that you want different things out of life. They can accept that Mommy or Daddy made some big mistakes, and now it's hard for the two of you to stay together.

But what they can't accept, and what hurts them, is a story that shifts. Or a story that puts one parent in a bad light. Or stories that conflict.

You're getting a divorce for yourselves. That's okay. But *how* you go about it has to be for your child.

And by the way, you do not "warn" your child that you *might* be getting a divorce. This is just going to scare your child and give him an inappropriate sense of responsibility that is far too great a burden.

YOU NEED TO THINK ABOUT HOW THE TWO OF YOU TOGETHER WILL ANSWER ALL OF THE PRACTICAL "WILL I BE OKAY?" QUESTIONS. She's going to want to know where she will live. What's going to happen to the dog? Where will she go to school? When will she see her friends? Who's going to pick her up after school? If she has a computer at your house now, will she have two computers, one at each house? Will she have two sets of clothes? Will her teachers have to know about this? Will she be able to call both parents whenever she wants? What happens when she needs something that's at the house where she's not staying?

Now you can't possibly prepare for all your child's questions. And you don't need to. But you do need to have a clear vision of what it's going to be like after you separate so you can sketch it in for her.

There is one more thing when it comes to planning for practicalities, and this is important. Whenever possible and wherever appropriate, consult your child and get her input about what she wants. The more say she has in little things, the easier it will be for her to get through the transition and feel safe.

For example, what color does she want the walls of her room to be? If she's going to be living with Mommy during the week, does she want Mommy to drive her to school on Monday? Because if she does, then Daddy needs to bring her home Sunday night. Any age-appropriate choice you can give a child will increase her sense of well-being.

YOU HAVE TO PLAN WHAT YOU'RE GOING TO DO TO MAKE YOUR CHILD FEEL SECURE EMOTIONALLY. Expect that your child will initially be upset. It's okay that he's upset. It's normal. You can't be upset about his being upset.

So don't try to make his feelings go away. Validate his feelings. Say things like "I know this is hard for you"; "I know you're scared"; "I know you're angry at both of us." Then encourage him to talk about his feelings.

But understand that he may not want to. Often kids need to process what's happening on their own. Don't be concerned if he does this. Just let him deal with things on his own timetable.

Encourage him to ask both of you a lot of questions. Expect that he'll ask some of the same questions over and over again. The more times you can give the same answer to the same question, the more quickly he'll be reassured.

AND MAKE SURE THAT YOU TELL THE TRUTH. Of course you have to tailor the truth you tell to the child's age. For a four-year-old, you have to keep it very simple. For a fourteen-year-old, you can go into more detail. But remember, by telling your child that you're getting a divorce, you've rocked his world. He doesn't need to have his world rocked yet again by some thin sugarcoating you've put on a story that will quickly wear off and reveal a very different truth underneath.

If, for example, he's not going to see as much of Daddy after the divorce, then you have to prepare him for that. You can make him feel better by saying that Daddy will always be in his life and always love him. But you should never say that one thing is going to happen when you know that it is going to turn out another way.

AS A KEY PART OF MAKING YOUR KID FEEL EMOTIONALLY SECURE, DON'T PUT HIM IN THE MIDDLE OF YOUR ANGER AND DISAPPOINTMENT WITH EACH OTHER. This is one of the most important principles, and one of the most often violated. Let me be blunt. Just because you think your spouse is a jerk, you should never make your kid think his parent is a jerk. All that would do is double his loss. He's lost an intact family, and now he's losing the sense that his parents are both okay people.

Why in the world would you ever want to do that to your kid? No matter how much you hate your ex, it's in your kid's best interest for him to hear from you that his other parent is a good parent, even if it's your private opinion that your ex could be a much better parent.

This is not just good for your kid. It's good for you, too. I've noticed something very interesting as I've followed families post-divorce: The parent who talks the most trash about the other is usually the one the kids get most disgusted with in the end.

Here's how this works. It makes your kid uncomfortable to hear you trashing his other parent. He knows on an emotional level that you're taking something away from him. So how can he not resent what you're doing? And this is especially true since the trash you're talking contradicts his own direct experience.

Let me lay it out for you. Don't trash each other in front of your kids. Don't have arguments with each other in front of your kids about issues that concern them, like who pays for what. Don't give your child the third degree after he spends time with his other parent. Don't use your child as a way of hurting the other parent. And don't use your child as a messenger for your relationship issues with each other. Just don't do any of these things.

But, parents sometimes ask, what do I do if I find out that my ex is talking trash about me?

I've got a great solution. Don't talk trash back. But here's what you *can* do. Remember that your kid is going through a disorienting experience. So you can become the voice of perspective, the person who makes sense of things for your child.

When your kid comes to you and says "Mommy/Daddy said you were a #%$&#," you could say something like "You know, when mommies and daddies divorce, sometimes they get so mad at each other that they just want to lash out and hurt each other, even though they know it's wrong." Now you've become the safe, comforting person your kid will see as a resource. This is good for you and good for your kid.

And, in case you want to know the secret of becoming the more popular parent, here it is. It's not being the parent who trashes the other the most. It's not being the most lenient parent. It's not being the parent who buys the best gifts. It's nothing like that.

Instead, the most popular parent is the one the kid can talk to most easily, and the one the kid feels most comfortable with. And the funny thing is that these are also qualities highly correlated with good parenting.

ONCE YOU'VE BOTH AGREED ON A "STORY," AND ON HOW YOU'RE GOING TO DEAL WITH YOUR CHILD'S NEEDS, *THEN* IT'S TIME TO TELL HIM ABOUT THE SEPARATION. You should tell your child at a time when something good has just happened, like when they've just eaten some of their favorite foods, and when there's going to be plenty of time to sit and answer questions and deal with emotions. It should be at a place where you will have uninterrupted privacy.

Resist the urge to make a long speech. Just say something like "I know you've heard Mommy and Daddy fighting a lot recently [or whatever it is your kid might have seen]. We've done everything we can to try to work out our problems, but we couldn't solve them, and our marriage just doesn't work for us anymore. So Mommy and Daddy have decided to live in separate places. This happens all the time, as you know, and you'll come to see that it all works out just fine. You'll be fine, and we'll all be fine.

"Here's what else you need to know. We both love you very much and we're always going to love you.

"And you need to know that you're always going to be the most important part of both of our lives, and you're always going to be with each of us and spend lots of time with each of us.

"And you need to know that what's happening is no one's fault. It's not our fault. And most important, we need you to know that in no way, shape, or form is it *your* fault. You're a great kid, and we'll both always love you and take care of you."

Then let your child know that you're sure she has lots of questions and a lot of feelings about this, and that you want to sit down with her so you can deal with everything she has in her mind and heart, either right now or whenever she wants.

To make her feel comfortable sharing all her fears and questions with you, you might say something like, "I wouldn't be surprised if you felt angry with us, or scared. But whatever you're feeling, it's okay. You just need to know that we're both okay with this. We really think that this is what's best for everyone. We're here to take care of you now. You don't have to worry about taking care of us. Everything is going to be okay. Your Mommy and Daddy will always be your Mommy and Daddy."

Be prepared for anything. Sometimes kids surprise us by having absolutely nothing to say. That's okay. Don't push them. If they have nothing to say, it's either because they're so surprised that they don't know how to begin to respond, or because they've seen it coming and they're very angry, or they don't know how to process their feelings yet.

But in most cases they do have questions. Remember, they're just kids. They're surprisingly ignorant about how the world works. You can never predict what they're going to ask or what they'll misunderstand. As long as you answer honestly to the level of their understanding, and at the same time focus on reassuring them that they'll be okay, you'll be doing a good job.

It's common for kids to talk about the two of you getting back together. Often your child will heart-wrenchingly make all kinds of promises she thinks might help the two of you get back together.

So that her trust is not further damaged, this is a time to be very clear and very honest. If you really are just separating and don't know if you're getting a divorce or not, then say so. But make it absolutely clear that there's nothing your child can do to affect your decision.

But if you are getting a divorce, then please don't offer false hope. It just confuses your child and makes her feel responsible for something that has nothing to do with her. The answer to her question is "No, honey, Mommy and Daddy have done their best, but now we know for sure that we don't want to stay together anymore. I'm sorry, but we're not getting back together. But we'll always love you and take care of you, and you'll always have everything you need."

You need to deal with your own feelings of guilt and worry during this process. The best way to deal with them is to think of this as a kind of emotional Outward Bound experience for your kid. It may be scary and difficult in the short run, but if it's handled well it will build their understanding and resilience. It will make them tougher, wiser people.

BE PREPARED TO DEAL WITH THE AFTERMATH. Making "the announcement" is the beginning, not the end, of helping your child deal with your divorce. Often children regress during this period. All this means is that they start acting in ways you'd thought they'd outgrown. Sometimes they wake up at night with nightmares and want to get into your bed. Sometimes the stress they're under makes them seem stupid or slow.

The only way to deal with this is to be patient. They'll be fine once two things happen.

First, they need to process everything that's going on, either in their own little heads or by talking with you.

Second, they need to have actual experiences that show, when the dust has settled, things really will be the way you've promised, and they really will be okay. This might take a year to work through. Give your child the gift of your patience during this transition.

Spend as much time as you can with your child. All the promises in the world can't compare with you actually being there as much or more than you have been.

I've talked a lot about making your child feel okay about the divorce and being sensitive to her needs. At the same time, however, it's important not to spoil your child. If she's had chores before, she should be expected to continue to do them. Whatever the rules have been before, you should continue to maintain those rules.

And, please, for the sake of your child, don't let guilt or desire to win her affection lead you to bribe her with gifts or to indulge her in other ways, other than making her feel loved and giving her the gifts of your time and patience.

■   ■   ■

I've outlined here how to do all this well. Don't worry, you're not going to do it perfectly. There are no perfect divorces. Things always get a little messy. But if you see that it's very hard for one or both of you to stick to what I've outlined, then, please, for the sake of your child, go into some kind of family therapy or work with a good child psychologist to make agreements between the two of you for how you're going to coparent in the best interest of your child.

Finally, be aware of the messages you're conveying to your child. You may very well be feeling scared and guilty. That's normal. But your child will pick up cues from you that will tell him what this means and how it's supposed to affect him.

Of course let him know that all his feelings and questions are normal and welcome. *But most of all, keep giving him the message that he's strong and resilient; that he'll come out of this okay; that everyone is going to be okay; that even though things are different, he still comes from a good, strong, healthy family.*

P 103 NEEDY — EFFECTIVE
KNOW WHAT YOU
WANT US WHAT person
CAN GIVE.